T0283748

on track ...

AC/DC

every album, every song

Chris Sutton

sonicbondpublishing.com

Sonicbond Publishing Limited
www.sonicbondpublishing.co.uk
Email: info@sonicbondpublishing.co.uk

First Published in the United Kingdom 2024
First Published in the United States 2024

British Library Cataloguing in Publication Data:
A Catalogue record for this book is available from the British Library

Copyright Chris Sutton 2024

ISBN 978-1-78952-307-2

The right of Chris Sutton to be identified
as the author of this work has been asserted by him
in accordance with the Copyright, Designs and Patents Act 1988.
All rights reserved. No part of this publication may be reproduced, stored in a
retrieval system or transmitted in any form or by any means, electronic, mechanical,
photocopying, recording or otherwise, without prior permission in writing from
Sonicbond Publishing Limited

Typeset in ITC Garamond Std & ITC Avant Garde Gothic
Printed and bound in England

Graphic design and typesetting: Full Moon Media

Follow us on social media:
Twitter: https://twitter.com/SonicbondP
Instagram: www.instagram.com/sonicbondpublishing_/
Facebook: www.facebook.com/SonicbondPublishing/

Linktree QR code:

For Belinda and Brent Fleming

Author Notes

Interviewees

Many were asked, but the following are those who agreed to contribute to varying degrees. Their thoughts and opinions remain theirs alone. My grateful thanks to Michael Browning, Peter Clack, Tony Currenti, Mike Fraser, Gerard Huerta, Ian Hampton, Noel Taylor and Dave Thoener. Where no other source is mentioned, all quotations are taken from these interviews.

The Australian albums

The Australian releases are the closest in integrity to AC/DC's vision for each album. The international releases differ in track choices up until *Powerage*, while the album covers were also changed, often completely, up until *Highway To Hell*. This infuriating state of affairs ended with the Bon Scott era. From *Back In Black* onwards, there was uniformity at last.

Although the official remaster series used the international releases, we are taking a purer route in this book through the albums, following the Australian releases. These albums, for the most part, are how they were originally conceived to be by the band. The differences between those albums and the international releases will be discussed following each related Australian release.

on track ...
AC/DC

Contents

Introduction
The Essence Of AC/DC
The secret to their success has always been their solid authenticity, with no frills or pretentiousness. This is a rock 'n' roll band, pure and simple, undiluted by trends. The Bon Scott era, with some noteworthy exceptions, defined their three main lyrical interests as sex, drinking, and rock 'n' roll – note, *not* drugs! The long era since then, with Brian Johnson, has seen no major change to this gold standard, except that the wordplay is less adroit. The songs are generally simpler in approach than with Bon!

At the heart of the sound have been the guitars of the Young brothers: Angus Young and his Gibson SG, alongside Malcolm and his trusty 1963 model Gretsch Jet Firebird. Mix in the human metronome that is Phil Rudd and Cliff Williams's pulse-beat bass lines, and you have the classic AC/DC sound. If you were to distil it down even further, you would surely be looking at the titanic rhythm playing of band 'governor' Malcolm, who lived and breathed rock 'n' roll. It's an enormous testament to the character and playing of Stevie Young that the band could continue at all after Malcolm's departure.

The Importance Of Family
Although founded in Australia, many of the early band members were immigrants from the UK, most notably, Bon Scott and the Youngs, all of whom hailed originally from Scotland. Bon was born Ronald Belford Scott in Forfar on 9 July 1946. His parents, Charles 'Chick' Scott and Isabelle 'Isa', emigrated to Melbourne from their home in Kirriemuir in 1952, taking Bon and his brother Derek with them. They sailed on the *Asturias* from Southampton on 5 March 1952, arriving 25 days later on 30 March in Fremantle, Perth. They initially stopped with Eleanor Laing (Isa Scott's sister) at 89 Couch Street, Sunshine, Victoria. It was while at school in Melbourne that he acquired the nickname Bon (for 'Bonnie Scotland'), which would stay with him for the rest of his life. The Scott family left Melbourne, after four years there, to live in Fremantle, Western Australia.

It was a tough working-class background for William and Margaret Young and their children at number 6 Skerryvore Road in the Cranhill area of Glasgow. The newspaper adverts promising a better new life in the sun proved irresistible. So, William and Margaret took the plunge and emigrated with four of their children by plane to Australia in May 1963. Their first home at the Villawood Migrant Hostel in Sydney turned out to have similar rough edges to their roots back in Glasgow. Speaking to *The Coda Collection* in 2003, Malcolm Young recalled the move to Australia:

> Glasgow got bombed quite extensively in World War II, and it never really recovered. Unemployment was high, and you could get to Australia for about £20. That was for the whole family to fly over. Not everybody left. Me and Angus were the youngest, so we went along with George. My sister

(Margaret Horsburgh) came with her husband and their young kid at the time. There wasn't a lot to do in Australia unless you liked sports.

The direct musical influences on Malcolm Mitchell Young (6 January 1953 – 18 November 2017) and Angus McKinnon Young (born 31 March 1955) came from their father William and older brother, George. Malcolm recalled the musical background to *The Coda Collection* in 2003:

Dad didn't play an instrument, but he would tap-dance and play the spoons. He had rhythm. On my mum's side, she had a nephew in Germany who played piano. All the brothers played acoustic guitars. A lot of Big Bill Broonzy songs. One of 'em used to play Scottish songs on the squeeze box. There always seemed to be instruments in the house. Angus and I picked up the guitar, like learning how to walk, as soon as we could. We'd see our older brothers knock up a tune, so we learned how to do it. We were basically brought into the world with guitars.

Older brother and mentor George Redburn Young (6 November 1946 – 22 October 2017) achieved success with The Easybeats in the 1960s. He got started at the Villawood Migrant Hostel: 'To pass the time, the kids would go to the recreation hall and play table tennis and strum guitars and so on. That's basically where the Easybeats started' (*Friday On My Mind, The Story Of The Easybeats*).

George's songwriting skills and the production talents that he learned, along with his close partner in The Easybeats, Harry Vanda, gave the duo a second career after the demise of their band. Vanda and Young, as they became better known, were the guiding lights for AC/DC and George remained on hand for advice to Angus and Malcolm till the day he died. It wasn't just about music; it was about family. The Youngs have always relied on each other and turned to family members for support, and you get a sense that everyone else in their world is very much outside of that circle. I put this to their former manager Michael Browning, who tactfully concurred that 'the Youngs are a very tight-knit family'. It was, and still is, an admirable strength.

Two older siblings also went on to work in the music business. Stephen Crawford Young (26 June 1933 – 13 December 1989) worked as part of the AC/DC organisation. He also emigrated to Australia in 1963 with his wife Janet and two sons. His oldest son is Stevie Young (born 11 December 1956), who went on to replace his uncle Malcolm in AC/DC. Alexander Young (28 December 1938 – 4 August 1997) played bass and saxophone under the pseudonym George Alexander with a UK-based band called Grapefruit. He later worked for Proud and Loud Management, based in Hamburg, who unsurprisingly had business dealings with AC/DC. He also wrote a song that AC/DC nearly recorded.

Tales Of Old Grand-Daddy – Marcus Hook Roll Band (1973)

Personnel:
George Young: vocals, guitar, bass, piano
Harry Vanda: vocals, lead guitar
Alan Waller: bass, vocals, piano
Angus Young: guitar (album and possibly third single)
Malcolm Young: rhythm guitar, lead guitar (album and third single)
John Proud: drums (album and third single)
Alex Young: tenor saxophone on 'Louisiana Lady' (single)
Howie Casey: saxophone (singles)
Freddie Smith: drums (first two singles)
Ian Campbell: bass (first two singles)
Produced by Wally Allen at Abbey Road Studios, London, between June and November 1972 and EMI Studios, Sydney, between July and August 1973
Release date: 1973
Label: EMI
Highest chart places: Australia: 89, UK: -, USA: -
Running time: 39:51
All songs by Harry Vanda and George Young except as noted

Malcolm recalled to *The Coda Collection* in 2003 the steps towards forming a band with Angus:

Angus and I had silent dreams about playing in a band. We played every day, and when George was around, we'd play with him too. We weren't competing with each other. We practised on our own, sorting out our styles. We never really played together. I was more into The Beatles and The Stones, and Angus was more into the heavier stuff, Hendrix and Cream, with the lead guitar. I used to listen to songs as songs – the drums, the vocal, the music side of it. I tended to pick up on the chords, the whole picture around the guitar. It just happened when I was putting together a band; we were going to get a keyboard player, but I got Angus instead. Angus had his own band, a little rock outfit, but they just packed it in. He told me they were finished, and I said, 'Come down tomorrow and have a bash'. We were going to play rock 'n' roll; it was as simple as that.

At this point, it's worth noting that Malcolm Young's legendary rhythm guitar playing has direct routes in big brother George's stellar work with The Easybeats, something else that Malcolm learned from him.

Malcolm and Angus's first recordings came not with AC/DC, but as part of a project George Young was working on. George and his fellow musical partner, and also a former Easybeat, Harry Vanda, had hooked up with Alan

Waller from The Pretty Things. Originally, Marcus Hook Roll Band was a London-based project that came together for two singles – 'Natural Man' and 'Louisiana Lady'. When an album was mooted, Vanda and Young were keen to record it in Australia with a session band. It's likely that George had Malcolm already in mind to play on it, and Angus wasn't far behind in his thoughts. Malcolm had already been in a band of some note. He joined The Velvet Underground (Sydney version) in 1971. By the time they changed their name to Pony in 1972, Malcolm was on his way out looking for a band that better suited his outlook and ambition.

The Australian album sessions commenced with the core band of Allan Waller, Harry Vanda, George and Malcolm Young and John Proud. Alan Waller described the set-up for the Australian sessions to *Billboard* in 2014:

At first, Malcolm and Harry were playing (guitar) and George started playing the bass. After a couple of days, Malcolm was really coming on brilliantly; he sounded like he should be about 30 or 50 years old 'cause he had so much maturity in his playing. I said to George one night, 'Your kid brother is something. He's great'. And he said, 'There's another one like him at home. You wouldn't believe it'. So, the next day, he showed up with Angus as well, and he was astonishing. He must've been 15 or 16 or something; he looked like a fresh-faced kid, but he played like a monster. So he would come along now and again, too. I think George wanted to let them know what it was like working in the studio. Malcolm was around the whole time, and Angus showed up occasionally.

The sessions went well. Waller tantalisingly added to *Rolling Stone* in 2014 that there had been a surfeit of material:

The Youngs are an incredibly talented family and an absolute joy to work with; no egos, no rubbish, just a 'good vibe' throughout the recordings. I came back from Australia with way too much material for an album, and after I'd finished mixing everything at Abbey Road, it was difficult to know what to leave out.

The fundamental point – that it was largely two different bands in London and Australia – was lost on *Rolling Stone*, who held up 'Louisiana Lady' (in 2014) as a focal track to hear early Angus and Malcolm, despite neither being on it! The album title is a reference to Jim Beam Old Grandad bourbon whiskey, which Waller brought into the sessions as liquid encouragement! The original cover had a certain charm that fitted the title but was replaced for the reissue CD in 2014 with a misleading AC/DC *Black Ice* style cover. It's an album worthy of investigation because the roots of Harry Vanda and George Young working together with Malcolm, and to a lesser degree Angus, are right here. The core album band also features future AC/DC drummer John Proud on drums. As well as the album there was also a single release of 'Can't Stand The Heat' with a non-album B-side. The reissue CD pulled together all the singles, the album, plus some session outtakes.

'Can't Stand The Heat'
It's an R&B chugger with a catchy chorus, but there's not a lot going on of interest other than a brief 'morse code' guitar part. The prominent saxophone is rather distracting. This was also released as the third single.

'Goodbye Jane'
Bright screeching guitar notes open this one before it settles into a steady chugging riff. The chorus is not far off being something Slade would have come up with and it has a positive good-time feel. The lead guitar sounds like it could be Malcolm and the rhythm track has some real energy to it. The piano-led outro takes things into boogie-woogie territory.

'Quick Reaction'
The melody of 'T.N.T'. can be heard in the chorus here, which implies that George Young had a lot to do with the writing of that song as well. There's a real Rolling Stones 'Honky Tonk Women' feel on the verses. George and John Proud are great on the rhythm, along with either Malcolm or Harry Vanda on rhythm guitar. It sounds like Malcolm's style and might well be him taking the solo, too. It's one of the best songs on the album.

'Silver Shoes And Strawberry Wine'
Time to slow things down for a reflective, slow blues ballad that reminds me of UFO. Waller sings it well in a light, bluesy style. There's a fluid blues-based guitar solo to match, which works well with a heavily strummed acoustic guitar backing it. It's followed later by rasping saxophone and squealing lead guitar duelling all the way to the outro. This excellent song is well worth hearing.

'Watch Her Do It Now'
The glam feel returns, but it falls short in terms of how powerful it might have been. The vocals let it down, being a bit too understated. The slide guitar part is rather distracting and wasn't the best choice for the song. It doesn't enhance the music in any way.

'The People And The Power'
This is the best song by far and Harry and George knew it. They later offered it up to their former Easybeat comrade Stevie Wright for his excellent album *Black Eyed Bruiser* (1975) – see *Appendix 2*. This version is looser than Wright's but still effective. There are twin guitars on both rhythm and lead, so Malcolm, at least, is involved. George's bubbling bass

runs are melodic and John Proud's cymbals sizzle satisfyingly. The solos are great, too, especially the saxophone.

'Red Revolution'

This track has a thicker sound. The verses have a Thin Lizzy quality with the twin guitar riff, not unlike Lizzy's later 'Don't Believe A Word'. The choruses have an early T. Rex glam/ hippy vibe in the style of their 'Hot Love'. Curiously, it incorporates a reprise of the lyrics of 'The People And The Power', which relates perfectly to the subject matter of carrying on as best you can under the oppression of 'the man'.

'Shot In The Head'

This is one of the closest to AC/DC territory. The rhythm and overlaid lead guitar have a dirtier, riff-heavy sensibility than much of the album. The slide guitar part adds some welcome extra texture and there are some effective lead guitar solos. The song stands up well to repeated listening.

'Ape Man'

One of the heavier songs. The main riff is very similar to Bad Company's later 'Feel Like Making Love', which is no bad thing by any means. Sadly, there's little other than that to admire. They stick to the riff and rhythm in what is a very simple song, where they successfully go for a simple, primal thud to suit the title.

'Cry For Me'

The album's closer is another ballad. An odd way to go out because its plaintive lyrics wear thin. It's pretty indistinct musically, too, other than the lead guitar solos, which sound like two different players trading off licks. Who the players are is unknown, but it's two of Harry Vanda, Malcolm and Angus. This could have been a better song with more dynamics to it.

Related Tracks
'Natural Man'

The first single by the London-based band has a bass pulse and some guitar riffs, which would later turn up in 'Live Wire'. The choppy rhythm chords, courtesy of George Young, are very AC/DC.

'Boogalooing Is For Wooing' (Alan Waller)

This R&B number, with plenty of energy, was the B-side of 'Natural Man'. There's nothing of note to it. Waller's material is pretty derivative and lacks the touches and melodic flair of Vanda and Young's work.

'Louisiana Lady'

The second single by the London-based band is a muscular driving rocker with a catchy chorus. You can really hear the Easybeats pop sensibilities in it and the song crackles with energy. It also benefits from a wild lead saxophone part by Alex Young.

'Hoochie Coochie Har Kau' (Waller/ Waller)
The B-side of 'Louisiana Lady' sounds like a poor Paul McCartney B-side or out-take. It's dreadful.

'Moonshine Blues' (Alan Waller)
The B-side to 'Can't Stand The Heat'(the third single) is one we have some firm information on for the credits. Waller worked on it in London and brought it with him for the Sydney sessions. Harry Vanda added the raw lead vocals, Malcolm added the guitar and George played bass. It's not a great song; it all sounds too polite and contained. But it's nice to hear Malcolm's lead guitar fills and solos.

'One Of These Days'
An outtake from the Sydne-y album sessions. Harry and Malcolm have been directly credited on guitars and George as the bass player on this one. Oddly, this great little song is better than anything that made the album. The lead guitar fills are terrific and the choruses and verses are strong. There's some wah-wah guitar for added colour. It all hangs together really well.

'Ride Baby Ride'
Another Sydney sessions outtake. All the guitars are played by Harry and George. The latter also sings it in his own inimitable talkie style, which he would later use with Flash And The Pan. It's pleasant and sounds like a fun Lynyrd Skynyrd-type song, but it's not one you rush back to hear again.

The Beginnings Of AC/DC
The name of the band came from their older sister, Margaret Horsburgh. She saw the initials AC/DC (which stands for 'alternating current/direct current') on a sewing machine. Malcolm and Angus loved the name, which, to them, summed up exactly the energy they were going for.

They appointed Denis Loughlin as band manager, who occasionally stood in for vocalist Dave Evans if he had to miss a gig. Their official debut performance was on 31 December 1973 at Chequers Club in Sydney. Dave Evans recalled the night to *VWMusic* in 2021:

> It was the most prestigious gig in Australia – to be doing New Year's Eve – going through midnight and counting in the new year. That was our first show and people were excited about us because of Colin Burgess in the band and because of Malcolm and Angus, the younger brothers of George. It was an amazing show and I'll never forget it. We started off with a bang.

Burgess's 'prestige' was down to him having been a member of successful Aussie band Master's Apprentice, while the link to George Young and The Easybeats was certainly a big draw.

While the band went on to conquer arenas and stadiums around the world, there are many fans who remain rightly nostalgic for the early days of the club and pub gigs. For that debut performance, the band consisted of Angus and Malcolm Young, Dave Evans (vocals, born 20 July 1953 in Carmarthen, Wales), Larry Van Kriedt (bass, born 4 July 1954 in San Francisco) and Colin Burgess (drums, born 16 November 1946 in Sydney). As the band gigged and built a following, the rhythm section kept changing. Finding the right combination appeared to have been a real problem. In mid-February 1974, they seemed to have settled on Neil Smith (bass) and Noel Taylor (drums). Taylor says, 'Me and Neil Smith were selected together to join the band' and he feels that in his brief time with them, 'AC/DC were a band looking for its individual presence in music and stage presence'.

In March 1974, the first known live recording of AC/DC surfaced. Taylor recalls that 'we had a residency at the Hampton Court Hotel in Kings Cross, Sydney, working on our repertoire, which included some originals. I recorded us at one show we did there. It's been bootlegged and is on the web, although I am not sure where my original copy is now'. The recording is of good quality and an important historical record of AC/DC, featuring several great cover versions. It's well worth seeking out. Taylor points out that it wasn't him who leaked the recording: 'Rumour has it that Dave Evans put it out, I only did a couple of copies. I never thought at the time that a recording I made on my little Aiwa tape deck for personal critique would be available to the world. I do chuckle!'

Part of the development of the band was Angus working on a formidable stage presence on lead guitar, dressed as a schoolboy. Malcolm credited his siblings, George and Margaret, for helping Angus, telling *The Coda Collection* in 2003 that:

> They thought a good act always had something people could relate to. My sister said, 'Why don't you get your school uniform with the shorts?' She knocked that up for him and this little guy became larger than life.

The school uniform struck Margaret as a good choice simply because she thought her brother looked cute when he would come home from school and play guitar in his uniform. It wasn't till April 1974 that Angus first appeared on stage in school uniform. The venue was Victoria Park in Sydney and Taylor recalls that the whole band had 'been thinking of wearing costumes because we thought it would get us noticed more'. Angus was already a focal point of the band and his costume enhanced that. The audience commented on it from that very first performance. He recalled to *Total Guitar* in 2020 that he walked onto the stage...

...the most frightened I've ever been, but thank God, I had no time to think. I just went straight out there. The crowd's first reaction to the shorts and stuff was like a bunch of fish at feeding time – all mouths open. I had one thing on my mind: I didn't want to be a target for blokes throwing bottles. I thought if I stand still I'm a target. So, I never stopped moving.

But while the other band members' costumes didn't last (see the photo pages), Angus's look caught on and it marked the band out. Taylor says that the band were now a distinctive live act:

Gigs were very interesting, to say the least. Angus looked the part in his schoolboy uniform, as it made him look 16 or 17. I seem to remember him not being allowed in through the front door at some venues for underage reasons. The audience were always interested in the band. Angus already had stage presence and was more than competent on guitar. Dave Evans played the rock star frontman with precision.

Angus's move to the lead guitar position was still a work in progress. Dave Evans pointed out to *VWMusic* in 2021 that, 'Malcolm was a better rhythm player; he was a strong rhythm player. When we first started, they both used to play lead. Angus wasn't the lead guitarist; he was one of the guitarists'. The band grew in strength with every gig and the audiences lapped them. Malcolm talked about their progress to *The Coda Collection* in 2003:

We had a good thing with the clubs. Rowdy, mad, brawling Aussies, it made Angus do it more. By the end of the night, everyone was won over. He wore the outfit, but he could play that guitar. We used to go to clubs and check out what was going on, and none of them were playing music that was getting people up and rocking and dancing. They didn't have a clue. It was just wide open for us. The very first show, the very first song we did, we had them won over. We'd play 'Jumpin' Jack Flash' and jam in the middle, drag it out, then some Little Richard, 'Great Balls Of Fire' and a couple more Stones tracks. Stuff we all roughly knew. Have a quick bash, and we just bluffed our way through. As long as they were up dancing, we were doing our job.

The band had a promo photo put together. Taylor recalls that 'It was made up from a photo shoot done at a gig on the top of a swimming pool centre at Broadway, Sydney. It was a regular outdoor gig for us at the time'. The promo photo indicated things were looking good for the band, but there were changes afoot. Malcolm wanted changes and, in April 1974, out went Noel Taylor and Neil Smith. Taylor didn't see it coming and recalls that...

...when Malcolm came to Neil and mine's residence to sadly inform us that we weren't the right rhythm section for the band, I was disappointed, but

Neil was relieved. Malcolm was sad it didn't work out because we got on really well. It was a short but sweet and memorable time. Malcolm was always confident of success for the band and the rest is history!

Rob Bailey came in on bass and Peter Clack on drums. The band were due to record a single, but the line-up on just two tracks recorded for the single was still fluid.

'Can I Sit Next To You Girl' b/w 'Rockin' In The Parlour' (1974) Single

Personnel:
Dave Evans: lead vocals
Angus Young: lead guitar on 'Can I Sit Next To You Girl, rhythm guitar on 'Rockin' In The Parlour'
Malcolm Young: lead guitar on 'Rockin' In The Parlour', rhythm guitar on 'Rockin' In The Parlour'
George Young: bass
Peter Clack: drums on 'Can I Sit Next To You Girl'
Colin Burgess: possible drums on 'Rockin' In The Parlour'
Produced by Harry Vanda and George Young at Albert Studios, Sydney, between February and May 1974
Release date: 22 July 1974
Label: Albert Productions
Highest chart place: Australia: 50
Both songs by Angus and Malcolm Young

George Young and Harry Vanda signed the band to Albert Productions, which they were a part of, and also came on board as AC/DC's producers. But who actually were the rhythm section on the single? Peter Clack says: 'It was Rob Bailey and me on 'Can I Sit Next To You Girl''. He adds that 'George played with me for six to eight weeks, and he taught me a lot – e.g. It's not always what you play but what you don't play! I didn't play on the B-side, which was recorded before I joined'. Clack joined the band in April 1974, so the A-side must have been recorded in April or later. Engleheart and Durieux (*AC/DC: Maximum Rock 'N' Roll*) say that the bass part was replaced by George Young, but they claim it was Larry Van Kriedt's part he replaced and *not* Rob Bailey's.

That leaves the B-side of 'Rockin' In The Parlour'. The probable pair in the rhythm section are Colin Burgess and George Young. According to Clack, the recording (circa February 1974) ties in with Larry Van Kriedt's brief tenure in the band on bass. Burgess was certainly experienced enough to record the drums, but George Young never thought long about replacing a bass part if he thought it needed it. It could well be him instead of Van Kriedt.

It is puzzling why there is a gap between the recording of the two songs, but a plausible explanation is that the A-side was intended to be 'Rockin' In

The Parlour', but they bumped it to the B-side while they worked up another song.

This is a fine enough debut offering, although it suffers in comparison to their later work. But if this had been all we ever had from AC/DC, it would be heralded as a lost, forgotten gem. Instead, it symbolises the first tentative steps of one of the greatest rock bands of our time. It's the only recorded output with Dave Evans and although he's a good singer, he doesn't have the power or strength of either Bon or Brian. For what the band wanted and where they were heading, they were right to dispense with his services.

We can thank Dave Evans for revealing to *VWMusic* in 2021 who played what on guitar:

> You got Angus playing lead guitar on 'Can I Sit Next To You Girl'. But on the B-side, you got Malcolm playing the lead on 'Rockin' In The Parlour'. We were on tour when Malcolm announced to us that he was going to stick with the rhythm because he was better at it than Angus. And, of course, Malcolm was writing the songs anyway at the time. He said that Angus was going to be the show pony, as it were, and do all the lead. That was Malcolm's decision.

There were, of course, other songs that could have been recorded. Dave Evans discussed two of them with *VWMusic* in 2021:

> There's one song called 'The Old Bay Road', which was a great song. They never ever recorded it, but we did it every night. There are one or two others. At the very first gig, I wrote a song called 'Sunset Strip' – on the spot. We didn't have enough songs, so Malcolm said, 'Just make something up'. So, I just introduced 'Sunset Strip' and Malcolm started a 12-bar rocker. We kept it in the set for the whole time that I was with the band. But after I split, they never recorded it.

Other known original unrecorded songs from the era include 'Midnight Rock' and 'Fell In Love'. The latter was reworked for the debut album.

'Can I Sit Next To You Girl'
This is nearly a minute shorter than the better-known version with Bon. The intro is completely different, displaying a bright (almost Joe Meek), shrill, poppy sound. Angus and Malcolm play off each other in a melodic guitar wrestle before this is broken, a mere 22 seconds in, by the band, as they launch into the familiar, almost Status Quo-like, riff. It still sounds too thin and Dave Evans' vocals are glam/poppy, which is a hard sell for those of us brought up on Bon and Brian.

In the rhythm section, Peter Clack is adequate, but George Young's melodic bass lines stand out. Angus picks up on them for his fills. His guitar sound, however, is a little shrill, lacking the fuller tone he is better known for. The other worthy mention is Malcolm, whose crunching rhythm guitar heralds the beginnings of the classic AC/DC sound.

'Rockin' In The Parlour'
The B-side opens with drums and cowbell, the Stones-esque intro being firmed up by a riff that The Cult would get close to on 'Lil Devil'. It's a very different AC/DC sound, far more poppy and lightweight, with only the rhythm guitar and Malcolm's lead guitar standing out in any way. Quite why they decided to choose the parlour as the venue for the 'action' is strange, to say the least. Not surprisingly, it was one they never came back to during the Bon Scott era.

The Highway To The Debut Album
AC/DC appointed Michael Browning as their manager in September 1974, the next step up on the road to success. He recalls his initial meeting with the band:

> I had the Hard Rock Cafe in Melbourne, which was a live music venue – no relation to the British Hard Rock Cafe chain. It was pretty much *the* live Melbourne venue at the time. All the Australian, and some international, bands played there. I had asked a friend of mine in Sydney if there were any bands from there I should be looking at to play at my venue and the name AC/DC popped up. I immediately pricked up my ears because I'd always been a fan of The Easybeats and, of course, George and Harry from The Easybeats were behind the band. So, they came and played for me when they were on their way to Perth and I thought they were great.

The Perth gig would mark the parting of ways with their manager Denis Loughlin (later to be lead singer with Sherbet). Browning wasn't surprised that things went so badly wrong in Perth:

> They had a guy (Loughlin) who was so cool managing them (he says sarcastically) that he booked them to Perth and then Adelaide on the way back. They arrived in Perth after driving over the desert; this was a long way, you know – like driving from New York to LA. They arrived there to discover they were booked to support a drag queen in a cabaret. So, the owner of the club obviously had assumed, with the name AC/DC, that they were some kind of gay band or something. So, they fired their manager and went to Adelaide.

Having sacked Loughlin, the band quickly found they were in dire straits. Cash, specifically the lack of it, was a pressing problem. They turned to Browning:

They were due to come back to Melbourne and play a bunch of dates, the Hard Rock cafe included, and they had run out of money. So they called me and asked if I would lend them some money. I said sure and they came and played my gig and that's where the conversation started about me managing them. I had been a manager of a very successful Australian band, Billy Thorpe & The Aztecs, and the band wanted someone who had a proven track record to take them over. So, me and my partner in the Hard Rock Cafe, Bill Joseph, financed them. We paid them a $60 per week wage each, resolved all their financial problems and gave them a road crew and a bus to travel around in. We got them a house to live in, too – we paid for everything. In return for that, we received all the money; that was the deal we struck up to consolidate them financially. After six months, it reverted to just a normal manager percentage commission scenario. So, we were very highly motivated to make it happen, to break them, within that six months so that we could not only pay their costs, but so we could actually make some money.

While Browning stabilised the band's operations, it was still clear that the band itself was still not right. Dave Evans became the next casualty, following his final dates in September 1974. Dave feels that money, not his vocals, was the main reason for his departure, as he told *VWMusic* in 2021:

We had a Top-Five hit record and we were doing the big shows there in Adelaide. And still, no money. We had a night off, and I confronted the manager (Browning) over this for all of us – not just for me. He smart-mouthed me and I stuck into him, and it was pulled apart pretty quickly; I didn't really hurt the guy. But that was it. I said, 'I want this resolved. I'm not leaving Sydney – I'm not doing all these shows unless I get paid something'. At the end of the tour, we had a meeting. They'd already talked and the manager was already pissed off. In the meantime, he'd spoken to Bon Scott to try to get him into the band because of what happened with me with him. My problem was not resolved, and so I split with the band because of that. That was the main reason.

Bon Scott came into the band's orbit via Vince Lovegrove, who ran the Jovan booking and management agency. Lovegrove took a call from George Young, enquiring if he knew of a singer. He had one right there as it happened. Living with Lovegrove at the time was his former Valentines bandmate Bon Scott, who was recovering from a motorbike accident. Lovegrove suggested Bon for the job, but George was uncertain on account of Bon still being unfit and, more importantly, his age.

At 28, he was indeed significantly older than his prospective bandmates and he had a history of bands behind him – including The Spektors, The Valentines and Fraternity. He was now 'resting', still hoping for the big career break. Angus tactfully recalled to *Total Guitar* in 2020 that 'Bon joined us pretty late in his life, but that guy had more youth in him than people half his age. That was how he thought, and I learned from him. Bon used to say to me, 'Whatever I do, you don't'.'

Bon's shared Scottish roots were surely a plus for the Youngs. They had a similar life experience and world view and they also had a shared admiration for one of Scotland's finest performers, Alex Harvey. Harvey also hailed from Glasgow (born 5 February 1935), and, like Bon, he achieved his major success when he hooked up with a younger band. Harvey was 37 when he joined up with Tear Gas in 1972, promptly renaming them as The Sensational Alex Harvey Band. The band's rise was, in large part, based on Harvey's charisma and his unique way with words and delivery. Bon Scott was a big fan and the parallels between the two are there to be seen and heard.

High Voltage (1975)

Personnel:
Bon Scott: lead vocals
Angus Young: lead guitar, rhythm guitar
Malcolm Young: rhythm guitar, backing vocals, lead guitar on 'Little Lover', 'Soul Stripper', 'You Ain't Got A Hold On Me' and 'Show Business'.
George Young: backing vocals, bass on 'Stick Around' and 'Love Song', percussion on 'Soul Stripper'
Rob Bailey: bass on all except 'Stick Around' and 'Love Song'
Peter Clack: drums on 'Baby Please Don't Go'
Tony Currenti: drums on all tracks except 'Baby Please Don't Go'
Harry Vanda: backing vocals
Produced by Harry Vanda and George Young at Albert Studios, Sydney, November 1974
Release date: 17 February 1975
Label: Albert
Highest chart places: Australia: 14
Running time: 39:51
All songs by Angus Young, Malcolm Young and Bon Scott, except as noted

High Voltage is where it all starts in earnest for the band's recording career, their first album for Albert Productions. Chris Gilbey, Vice President of Alberts, was confident in the band because of George Young's presence. He told *Double J Radio* in 2017 that:

> In the early period, George was a far greater controlling influence than any of the members of the band. Because George was the big brother and he'd been there with The Easybeats, he knew the ropes, he'd gone to England and he'd had hit records. I think he imparted a very strong ethic as to what the music business was about, what music was about and staying close to the roots. I think that was one of the things that George really communicated.

The songs were (mostly) ones that had been tried and tested on stage, including one cover version. Michael Browning says one was enough: 'We didn't want to start off recording covers. Malcolm was pretty much the main songwriter. When Bon joined, he was an amazing lyricist, so we had lots of songs quickly and away they went'.

It does enormous credit to Vanda and Young that the album feels like the work of one band, considering that the personnel in the rhythm section differs from song to song. In theory, the band was Bon, Angus, Malcolm, Rob Bailey (bass) and Peter Clack (drums). In the studio, both Bailey and Clack had their parts replaced on songs to a greater or lesser extent. Clack, in fact, is only heard on 'Baby Please Don't Go', replaced on everything else by Tony Currenti. Clack told *Sleaze Roxx* in 2021 how and why that happened:

It had to be done in a week and it had to be done at one o'clock in the morning. So, the only track that I got down was 'Baby Please Don't Go'. I had been playing every night and I just didn't have the stability or the constant reproduction. (George) came up to me and he said, 'Look, you're obviously pretty stuffed (tired). But do you mind if we have someone else fill in and I'll try someone else on some of the songs?'

The 'someone else' was already at the studios. Tony Currenti explains how the invitation came:

I was recording with my band and we finished recording at 11 o'clock. George approached me and said, 'can you hang around? The others are coming in and we'd like to record some songs and I'd like you to help them out'. I said, 'Yeah, why not'. The thing I always remember him saying was, 'If you can keep timing for four minutes, you can be the drummer'.

Currenti waited around with George Young till the band turned up: 'The first one coming in was Bon Scott. He was the only one in the band that I knew. He was very happy to see me and I was happy to see him. We stood there chatting a bit'.

That first night, Currenti recalls recording 'two songs, which were 'Little Lover' and 'Show Business'. I kept everything simple, and George liked that'. What was evident immediately that night to Currenti was how crucial George Young and Harry Vanda were: 'I think George was the architect of it (AC/DC). And Malcolm took over from him with sort of the same thing. George ran the members of the band; he was the organiser. But on the production side, the two of them worked together. George and Harry were a great combination'.

Currenti impressed George and the boys so much that 'I was asked to finish off the album. We did another two songs every night – four nights, eight tracks. I did seven tracks on the album, plus 'High Voltage'. That one got picked as a single, so it wasn't included on the album'. For clarity, Currenti confirms that 'with the exception of 'Baby Please Don't Go', I did the lot'.

The band liked Currenti's playing and personality, so they made him an offer (he could refuse):

They asked me to join the band, but I was involved with another band that had just finished a single. After recording a couple of nights, they approached me again and I thought about it some more because of the songs. They were great. But then another issue came up – Angus wanted to go to England pretty much yesterday. Because of having an Italian passport that restricted me from travelling, I thought I did the right thing by saying no because I wouldn't get out of Australia anyway. If I'd have had an Australian passport I would have said yes. But I am grateful to George and the boys for giving me the opportunity to record with them.

Former singer Dave Evans singled out Currenti to *VWMusic* in 2021 for
acclaim: 'Peter (Clack) just couldn't get that sound that Malcolm wanted. So,
they ended up using (Tony) on the first album as a session player. He just
played what he was told to play, and he got that drum sound on the first
album that everybody knows'.

One who was surprised by Currenti playing on the album and the offer to
join was Michael Browning: 'Quite honestly, Tony Currenti's name never came
up with me. The first I ever heard about him was a few years or so ago'. He
admits, though, that 'I was pretty much the kind of manager who kept away
from what was happening in the studio. That all happened in Sydney, and I
was in Melbourne'.

The album features two bass players. Most of the bass is handled by band
member Rob Bailey, while George Young tackled the rest. Currenti is certain
of what George played on: 'There's only three songs that George played: 'Stick
Around', 'High Voltage' (non-album) and 'Love Song'. All the rest got done by
Rob Bailey'. While Bailey acquits himself well with a simpler style that nods
towards future bass men Mark Evans and Cliff Williams, George's playing was
substantially different. Currenti explains that 'George played bass like a lead
guitar; he had a melodic way of playing. That was made possible by Malcolm
playing rhythm. Malcolm played rhythm like a bass player, so the bass player
could venture around like a lead guitar. I thought it was very fascinating'.

As well as Vanda and Young, huge credit must also be given to the core
band trio of Angus, Malcolm and Bon. They really rise to the occasion and
deliver. Even on what is sometimes less than stellar material, you can hear
and feel that something special is coming together. Bon's confidence oozes
out of the speakers and the Angus/ Malcolm guitar machine is already
developing well. As noted, Malcolm plays some lead as well as rhythm.
Comparing Malcolm's lead style to Angus, Currenti opines that 'Malcolm was
more melodic – I thought he was great'.

Malcolm would still play occasional lead guitar part further on down the
line, but never to the same degree he does here. He told *The Coda Collection*
in 2003 how he had envisaged the band's guitar sound developing:

I was more into the chord thing, the complete song, rather than the
individual part. I was glad, in a way, because I was more of a melodic player.
Angus was more into the rock world. Straight away, I said this is great. There
was never any question. I thought it was pointless for me to play solos. It
was never a brotherly squabble but the opposite because we just wanted to
do good as a band.

One who must have looked on with massive disappointment was Dave Evans,
especially as he recognised some of the songs as ones he had been working
on prior to them going in the studio, starting with 'Sunset Strip'. He outlined
this to *VWMusic* in 2001:

When they recorded *High Voltage*, they kept that arrangement, but Bon Scott changed the lyrics and it became 'Show Business'. The arrangement of the music was the music that we played to the original 'Sunset Strip'. And there's another song I wrote with them called 'Fell In Love', which we used to perform. Bon Scott changed the lyrics to that one and it became 'Love Song'. So, [Bon] changed the lyrics to two of my songs and recorded them. Those two were my songs originally; I wrote them with Malcolm.

They were not the only ones to get used and altered either. Evans continued ...

...of course, we had 'Can I Sit Next To You Girl'/ 'Rockin' In The Parlour'. Also 'Rock And Roll Singer' – I recorded that for the first album. 'Soul Stripper' was already recorded for the first album, as well as 'Little Lover'. So, we had five songs already recorded for the first album and were about to do 'Baby Please Don't Go', which I used to do with the band. But when Bon Scott joined the band, he got his chance and they re-recorded most of the stuff that I did. And he re-wrote the songs as well, so I was a bit pissed off about that. But that's life.

Evans' claim that there was an album underway with him as the vocalist seems to have missed being commented on elsewhere and it's hard not to think that those recordings were part of the reason for his dismissal. You can easily imagine George Young, for one, having strong opinions.

One big negative about the album is the cover. It's a nondescript cartoon-style image of a dog cocking its leg at an electrical substation. In its way, the basic and no-frills image mirrors the music within. However, it looks like a cheap album cover from an obscure band that never made it. It's fascinating that it's for a band set to explode onto the world stage.

Song-wise, the album is down-to-earth and relevant to their audience. There are no airs and graces and this is something they have resolutely stuck to throughout their career. AC/DC have always been a people's band. It's sometimes picked out as one of the worst of their albums, and the treatment of the songs on international releases doesn't help negate that view. But there are some effective songs and a deep classic in 'Soul Stripper'. Currenti agrees and points out how much the band had developed: 'We had the pleasure to play with them in Victoria Park when they were a Rolling Stones covers band. In the studio, when they were recording their original songs, I liked their material. 'She's Got Balls', 'Soul Stripper', 'Stick Around' – I thought they were all great songs. 'Love Song' is one of my favourites'.

The album title is excellent, accurately summing up the band, but it's confusing that what should have been the title track was not included and held back (as similarly did Led Zeppelin with 'Houses Of The Holy' and Queen with 'Sheer Heart Attack'). Currenti loved the title: 'There was a joke between me and George about the title – my name is Currenti, current/ high voltage and AC/DC are related to current, so I thought it was very appropriate', he laughs.

One thing that is firmly bedded in on the album is the AC/DC drum sound. Currenti feels that he was, in effect, the architect of the style. 'They based everything on that feel. Even Phil Rudd had to copy my style to do the next albums. Right up to *Powerage,* I think, because George wanted that style, so he (Phil) had to adapt to it'. The band still had some uncertainty over the drum stool position, carrying on with the man whom they hadn't considered good enough for the album. Currenti recalls that 'they kept Peter Clack in for a few months until they got Phil Rudd'.

From this decent debut album, AC/DC went on to global success. Currenti says that he could see it coming: 'After recording with them and hearing they were on a good level, I could see them making it all the way. They had Harry and George there; they had everything'.

'Baby Please Don't Go' (Big Joe Williams)
First track, first album and they absolutely nail this song. The band showcase their roots in what is a big statement of intent. It's the only song that actually features the full band who are supposed to be on the album. The Rob Bailey/ Peter Clack rhythm section does a great job here, right from the pulsating intro, which grabs your attention.

The guitars are a joy, with the brothers duetting on the riff, Angus's higher part wailing more than the lower rhythm from Malcolm. The underpinning bass/drums pulse is a contrast, with Bailey sticking to a simple, effective bass part alongside Clack's equally straightforward drums.

It's the first song with Bon, of course. His voice is clear and commanding; he totally sells the song with a level of clarity and power that he would gradually lose over the years as the alcohol and touring took their toll.

The frantic onslaught breaks down at 2:13. If it had stopped right there, that would have been enough – a short, sharp shock. Instead, they come back in for a breakdown section that sounds like it was recorded separately and edited onto the first half. It's an imaginative idea that takes the song up several notches. The insistent rhythm guitar is catchy and you get Angus throwing in some of what will become his trademark 'widdly' lead guitar fills. Bon gets to scat the lyrics in a call and response to some blues licks from Angus, too. There's just time for a headlong rush into a big ending, with Bon increasingly imploring his baby not to leave.

'She's Got Balls'
The inspiration for the song was Irene Thornton. She was Bon's wife, who he married in 1972 and separated from in 1974. A raunchy rhythm guitar riff from Malcolm opens it, soon doubled by Angus. It's a steady tempo, but Bon elevates the song to another level with his superb vocals. You can hear

he means it; he gets the tone and inflections just right describing Irene. Also, every line in the verses has a word he gives extra measure to (spunk, funk, speed, etc.). He then tops that with the emphatic chorus, which has, by contrast, some amusingly deadpan gang backing vocals.

Angus takes a great solo, which adds real flourish, but otherwise, the song stays in its respectful groove without getting over-excited. The outro would be pretty generic but for a second solo from Angus. It's a great little song, though.

'Little Lover'

The tempo drops right down for this slow groove. It's possibly the oldest song on the album; Malcolm was reported in *Classic Rock*, 2016 to have written the music when he was 14, with Bon adding new lyrics. Bon audibly enjoys every word of this homage to his 'little lover', relishing every line. Although some sources claim it is John Proud playing drums on 'Little Lover', according to Tony Currenti, it is definitely not: 'No, see there was a mistake made by George. He said in an interview that I played on *some* of the tracks because he was making way for Phil Rudd to be part of the band. John Proud wanted to be involved, but he never got asked. He was never in the picture'.

One problem with the song is the subject matter, which strongly implies an underage lover. That's not helped by Bon exclaiming that 'you had my picture on your bedroom wall next to Gary Glitter'. Now, he wasn't (one supposes) to have known about Glitter's predilections, but it's a pretty uncomfortable link with hindsight, given the lyrics.

That slow swaying groove is set from the outro, with Bon sounding like he's drooling and barely able to contain himself. It reminds me similarly of 'The Jack', too, especially in the way they shift gears from the verse up into the full-on chorus. Over the verses, the band keep it all very simple and low-key, which gives Bon the space to deliver his eulogy. The only break in it is the first solo on the album from Malcolm. It doesn't justify its length when it 'ends' abruptly at 4:50. But six seconds of silence later, there's a coda, which is actually the best part of the song. Some lovely dueling guitars brighten things up and it's great to hear the interplay between Malcolm and Angus.

'Stick Around'

This song fell under the radar for many fans, not being picked up for the international *High Voltage* compilation or the ridiculous *74' Jailbreak* one. It finally got an international release on the *Backtracks* box set.

The opening guitar riff over Currenti's drums is the first example of one of those simple blasting riffs that AC/DC do so well. The song then explodes when George's bass comes in and Angus's lead guitar wails. George's bass playing is always a joy to hear. His sense of melody is superb but he never overdoes it, adding interesting colour to the rhythm and another dimension to the sound. Malcolm sticks to the riff, leaving Angus to add fills and solos where he feels it. The long, drawn-out note he gets in at 2:50 makes sure you are paying attention! It's probably a bit too long, but it's a criminally underrated track. That lead bass and lead guitar combination is such a thrill, as is the outro with Angus's guitar soaring off into the distance!

'Soul Stripper' (Angus Young/ Malcolm Young)
It's the best track on the album and one of the finest early AC/DC songs. It was inexplicably ignored for the international *High Voltage* compilation album. Everything about this song is just pure class.

The bass in the intro is catchy and bouncy, with crashing guitar riffs. There's a lot of space between the instruments in the verses, with the guitars panned wide as the Youngs play call-and-response guitar lines. The extra percussion is mixed up high alongside Currenti's drums. It's George Young (Currenti confirms) adding the claves, bongos and, later in the song, tambourine.

It's such a compelling groove that you don't notice Bon is missing. He doesn't come in until 2:05 and he is so assured, delivering a strong conversational vocal as he recounts the story. The chorus is big, as though someone has plugged them directly into the mains. They just crash into it with juggernaut energy.

The middle of the song sees Bon drop out while the Young brothers trade more solo licks. First up is Malcolm at 4:03, followed by Angus at 4:11, etc. You can hear the difference in the sound of each guitar quite clearly. Malcolm even goes in for some two-handed tapping at 4:47 before the section winds up with Angus's last solo at 4:54. It's a great part of the song and shows what a great twin-lead band they could have been if they wanted. The big outro is pure Angus, as he runs riot while Bon repeats the title ad infinitum over the crashing rhythm track. Angus finishes with a strident guitar 'kiss' over an audibly happy band.

'You Ain't Got A Hold On Me'
This one sees Angus on rhythm while Malcolm handles the bluesy lead guitar parts. His style is not unlike Mick Ralphs, who plays in a similar vein on many Bad Company songs. The song itself is rudimentary, so it's fortunate that Malcolm lights it up – the solo he plays at 2:02 is a fabulous, sweet-toned piece of work. Otherwise, this is one of the lesser songs on the album.

'Love Song (Oh Jene)'
It was originally called 'Fell In Love', at which point it was a Malcolm Young/ Dave Evans composition. One who loves it is Tony Currenti: 'My favourite is 'Love Song'. It was different and there was more involvement. If I had joined the band, I would have hoped for more music in that sort of territory'. There's probably nobody else who would agree with him. It certainly is an anomaly on the album – it doesn't even sound like AC/DC. Angus picked it out to *Loudwire* (2020) as the song he most regretted recording:

That was very different for us. I didn't know if we were trying to parody love songs of the time because Bon wrote the lyrics. The guy who worked for us at our record label told us that that style was on the local radio at the time, very soft music. His thought (was) that we should release the song because it'll probably get some airplay. I remember thinking, 'Who in their right mind would want this to go out?'

The song does have a highly dramatic feel to it in the cinematic opening, which always reminds me of a horror film! Angus's spiralling intro riff leads all the way down the line to 'Thunderstruck'. It's also the best thing about the song. From there, it's downhill all the way into a turgid ballad. Bon, for one, doesn't sound at home on it; he just can't sell the song. Angus gets off a reasonable solo, but he is restricted by the tone and theme and has to operate within that format. It's practically a West Coast LA feel until they take things up for the outro when they get to show some teeth. Too little too late. It was obvious that this was a failed experiment.

'Show Business'
The song's origins go back to the Dave Evans-era 'Sunset Strip'. Bon reworked the lyrics. Currenti plays a drum roll in the intro leading into a Chuck Berry-style rocker, which is so authentic you would think it's actually an old song. Both of the Youngs handle rhythm guitar as well as the lead parts to great effect. The song itself isn't that great, being a little stuck in the rhythm track, but the solos are effective enough. It would take on a new lease of life in a live setting, where it became an explosive track.

What Happened Next?
On the back of the *High Voltage* album, the band increasingly appeared on TV while still gigging heavily and building up a big following. Browning recalls that:

In those days, there was a very healthy pub rock scene in Australia, and they played that circuit, but there was also a healthy pop scene. Not many people were aware that their demographic was mostly young teenage girls because they were on national television just about every second week on a show called *Countdown*. It was an Australian version of *Top Of The Pops,* if you like. So, they had major television exposure as pop stars and the girls would come to gigs and pull them off stage. It was hysteria. The pubs had rooms which held 1000 to 1500 people and they presented bands every night of the week. It elevated the group to a very successful situation in Australia.

A big part of the band's progress was getting a long-term rhythm section in place. First to join was former Buster Brown drummer Phil Rudd. He was born on 19 May 1954, the son of a German immigrant Hugh Witschke and his Irish wife Ivy Margaret (nee Boyle). Phil also had a sister, Marilyn Kaye Witschke. Both Phil and Marilyn took the surname of their mother's second husband Anthony Rudzevecius, which Phil, probably sensibly, shortened for his professional career!

Phil's contribution to AC/DC was immense from day one. If you had to bring it down to basics as to what sets him apart, it would be his metronomic timing and the incredible feel/groove he injects into his parts. A common touch he uses is playing slightly behind the beat. This is most noticeable on the slower tempo tunes and that's where the groove is felt. Then there's his great use of cymbals, especially his hi-hat work. He often doesn't go for the obvious hits, varying his approach. Take Phil Rudd out of AC/DC and it just isn't the same.

For a short time, the band were out touring without a regular bass player, leaving Malcolm to handle bass. On the occasions that George Young was free, he would cover bass duties, allowing Malcolm to go back to rhythm. But they knew they needed a new permanent bass player.

Mark Evans (born 2 March 1956 in Melbourne) told *Rocktopia* (2012) how he got the gig.

I was at the Station Hotel in Melbourne. An old pal of mine was there, a guy called Steve McGrath. He was actually working for the band and he said, 'These guys are looking for a bass player'. What got my attention was two of the guys in the band; their elder brother is George Young from The Easybeats. I was and always will be an Easybeats fan. That got my attention and I went around and met them. I got a copy of the record (*High Voltage*) and went back and played it the next day. Two days later, I was back with them at the Station Hotel. It all happened very quickly. The following week, I was on national TV (the *Countdown* show) playing 'Baby, Please Don't Go', with Bon dressed up as a schoolgirl!

Mark joined in March 1975 and was immediately put on the same $60-a-week wages as the rest of the band by Browning and Joseph. AC/DC had two roadies at this stage – Tana Douglas (the first female roadie, it is said) and the man Mark describes in his autobiography as 'Ralph The Roadie'. It was Ralph who gave him 'a friendly piece of advice': 'It's Malcolm's band, and it would be an excellent idea to remember that.

It's apparent that these were lively times for the band gigging around Australia and the band itself had some strong personalities. Browning laughs and comments that: 'Bon liked to party, but the rest of them were fine. Angus just wanted to go home and have a cup of tea. Phil was alright, you know, a good solid drummer. He fitted in with no problems, although there were problems later on. Certainly, in the very early days in Australia, when there was a huge female fanbase, there were a lot of shenanigans that went on, that's for sure'.

Evans played his first gig with the band on 20 March 1975 at the Waltzing

Matilda Hotel in Melbourne. Together, the Rudd/ Evans combo anchored the sound properly for the first time. This was the real beginning of the AC/DC sound. Time to record a new album.

T.N.T. (1975)

Personnel:
Bon Scott: lead vocals, bagpipes on 'It's A Long Way To The Top'
Angus Young: lead guitar, rhythm guitar
Malcolm Young: rhythm guitar, backing vocals
Mark Evans: bass on all except 'High Voltage' and 'School Days'
Phil Rudd: drums on all except 'High Voltage', backing vocals
George Young: bass on 'High Voltage' and 'School Days', percussion on 'It's A Long Way To The Top' and 'High Voltage'
Tony Currenti: drums on 'High Voltage'
Produced by Harry Vanda and George Young at Albert Studios, Sydney, April 1975
Release date: 1 December 1975
Label: Albert
Highest chart places: Australia: 2
Running time: 41:55
All songs by Angus Young, Malcolm Young and Bon Scott, except as noted

The band significantly upped their game from their debut with much better songs. This was evidenced when Atlantic's Phil Carson chose tracks from it and the debut for the international debut album *High Voltage*. He picked nine songs and seven came from *T.N.T.*

Evans commented on the songwriting to *Rocktopia* in 2012 and why there was a certain continuity, even after his time in the band:

> Angus and Malcolm have a history of writing a lot of lyrics, right back to 'Can I Sit Next To You Girl' and 'Rock 'N' Roll Singer'. It's completely natural; they're used to coming up with a lot of ideas. They used to work with Bon on the lyrics. There are people who say the lyrics after Bon are somewhat similar; well, the reason is that they have a long history of writing lyrics before Bon.

Credit also to Vanda and Young, who harness the band's live sound brilliantly on this album. Evans says that they spent two weeks in total recording the album. The first week was spent recording the backing tracks, with solos and vocals recorded the following week.

The band had used up all of their own original songs for *High Voltage*, so it meant that the bulk of *T.N.T.* was written in the studio. All they had prior to going in were a few riffs, such as the one for the title track. The process in the studio was to work up the parts on guitars before Malcolm and Angus sat down at the piano with George to firm up the tracks.

The album title is a poor one; it doesn't really hit the mark, being too simplistic and obvious. But there's nothing else that would have worked any better among the other track titles. It's worth noting at this point that AC/DC have always managed to avoid releasing a self-titled album, unlike most of their contemporaries.

The sleeve of this Australia/New Zealand-only album is as raw as the music. Two pieces of an exploded crate of T.N.T. lie on rough ground, each stamped in red with the band name and album title. The design is repeated for the back cover, with a panel for the song titles. More interesting is the inner bag, featuring lyrics and card catalogue 'police' files on each band member, with a snapshot attached. The way each photo is attached means that the date of birth of each member is, at least, partially obscured. The exception, surprisingly, is Bon, who might have had more reason to hide his date of birth!

T.N.T. is one of AC/DC's best and most consistent albums, with a solid core of five classic songs: 'It's A Long Way To The Top', 'The Jack', 'Live Wire', 'T.N.T' and 'High Voltage'.

'It's A Long Way To The Top (If You Wanna Rock 'N' Roll)'

George Young knew that Bon had played in a pipe band in his youth and thought bagpipes would add a lot of character to the song. Bon went out of the studio and returned with a set of bagpipes, which he had paid $479 (Australian) dollars for. It was a lot of money; enough, reckoned Evans (in *Dirty Deeds*), to have 'bought two Strats'. What George didn't know was that Bon had been a *drummer* in the pipe band. Before Bon got around to playing the pipes, there was the problem of setting them up. If that was hard, it was nothing compared to actually playing them! The end result is his best efforts looped on tape. It works well; the pipes take the song to a euphoric level and are a nice nod back to three of the band's roots.

You can't tell at all, but George constructed the song piece-by-piece from what was actually a studio jam. 'George is brilliant, he's the fucking best record producer', Evans enthusiastically told *Double J Radio* in 2017. 'George got the tape and cut everything in. The verses and the chorus are all the same. The song was never played in one piece in the studio; it was all cut together from one big jam. That was George Young; the guy is a genius'.

The opening riff from Malcolm is a classic – so clean and punchy, joined by Angus playing a harmony part a mere seven seconds in. Angus then adds a harmony at the end of each round of the riff until Bon comes in for the first verse at 0:30. He absolutely smashes the delivery on this - every inflection is just right. As he comes to the end of the first verse at 0:43, Angus plays a riff in response to each phrase – 'Gettin' robbed' (guitar), 'Gettin' stoned' (guitar), etc. – that gives it a touch of extra class.

Again, it's the spaces in the delivery that catch you, the slight pause before he sings, 'I tell you folks it's harder than it looks', and then wham-bam right into the chorus. The backing vocals are a little cursory and this is perhaps the one element of the song that needed more work. The bagpipes come swooping in at 1:25, adding an effective melodic counterpoint. They take the song up to a new peak and you have to smile when the call and response between Angus and the bagpipes enters at 1:55! Not content with that, Angus then solos over the end of each of the bagpipe phrases! It's back to the intro riff at 2:37, with the bagpipes slowly dying down to one long, low note that fades out. It clears the sound for the band to rock out, with extra percussion from George in the mix. The obvious big finish needed the bagpipes, so George fades them back up at 3:58. They blast out a two-note riff, with the band hammering the rhythm underneath.

This outstanding song should have had a longer run in the set and been an ever-present, in my opinion. The lack of bagpipes will be part of the reason why not, but you could get a stadium going mad on that riff and chorus alone! This is one of the very best songs they have ever recorded.

It was released in December 1975 (Australia only) as the second single from the album. They recorded a memorable video for it, showing the band on the back of a truck playing the song while travelling along Melbourne's Swanston Street.

'Rock 'N' Roll Singer'
A cooling off after the euphoria of track one. Despite that, there's real fire and grit in the riffs. The rhythm track really drives along, with Angus adding swaggering blues licks over it. Bon sounds like he is recounting his own backstory, such is his conviction. Bon's condemnation of the nine-to-five alternative work ethic is heartfelt. But, by contrast, it's delicious when he turns to the benefits of being in a band and gets in that emphasis on 'I hear it pays well'. The chorus is good, but they would get better at these in later years with more effective backing vocals. It's also a little overlong, but otherwise this is a solid piece of work which relies on that rhythm and Angus's thrilling lead work.

'The Jack'
Angus recalled the song's origins to *Guitar World* in 2000: "The Jack' is a song that came out of playing the pubs and clubs in the beginning. Bon would make references to a lot of people who had been his 'love companions' for a while. Bon, in his day, had a bit of a reputation'.

The live version has become so familiar that it's a surprise to hear the version on the album. The lyrics were rewritten to avoid offence and Bon, cleverly and adeptly, came up with multiple card game references inspired by the Jack in the title. This studio version is tauter and more economical than any of the live versions – and all the better for it. Angus's great solo is a blues burner in the style of Jimmy Page.

What you can hear in the chorus (which is the same as the live version) is the delight as they touch base with the 'true' version. There's an overlong section (from 4:07) where Bon sings, 'She's got the jack', and the band sing 'jack' back at him, eventually leading to only the band singing 'jack'. The song

35

could have done with some pruning to its overlong 5:53. Despite that, I prefer the studio version over the more rambling live version.

'Live Wire'

This classic has all the hallmarks of the best work of AC/DC to come. The opening fast bass pulse sets the tone, joined, after just seven seconds, by a strummed electric playing the melody. It rises up in volume till the 36-second mark when it really starts to crunch as Phil's cymbal comes in. The rhythm riff from here on is vintage AC/DC. The next killer part is when the second rhythm guitar comes in (at 0:51) and doubles the riff. The sheer power of this is electrifying. With Phil now turning to the drums, it's thrusting high-octane stuff.

Other singers might go for turbo-charged vocals to match the backing track, but not Bon. He enters after just over a minute with a measured opening vocal – 'Well, if you're lookin' for trouble, I'm the man to see'. His understatement makes him totally convincing.

The chorus is strong. Interestingly, they don't include backing vocals on the first one. Bon's retort of 'I'm a live wire' is answered purely by Phil's drums. The second chorus (2:33) introduces backing vocals, which sound like Malcolm alone. The bridge (2:47) changes the rhythm and sets up the guitar solo, which is a tautly constructed, almost restrained piece. Angus slows down his solo, picking out the notes, and nicely cues up the last verse and chorus. Bon is now well and truly let loose, even on the verse, and the chorus is a repeated blast, with Angus soloing away. It's a great song and one that really came into its own on stage, where it worked so well opening the show.

'T.N.T.'

When George Young heard Angus chanting along to the song in the studio, he suggested that he add his 'Oi!' chants to the track. 'I was never the greatest background singer in the world', Angus recalled in *AC/DC: Maximum Rock & Roll*. 'So, George said, 'Hey, this is more your cup of tea''.

One chord from Malcolm opens proceedings before Phil comes in. A swinging melodic rhythm and that 'oi' chant create a great base for Bon to work from. The spaces Bon leaves in his phrasing allows the rhythm guitar to 'pop up'. It works well because the riff isn't as heavy as you might expect from the title, being pretty light in tone. Credit to George Young as ever, who, as he so often would do, worked out how to get the swing and groove into the song. The three-second pause from Bon before the chorus sets it up well. But it doesn't have the extra power the song gets live and it's a shame they couldn't build it up more here. It's also noticeable how low the bass and drums are mixed on this track, which has a lot to do with that lack of power. Angus's solo (2:10) is suitably frenzied but somehow blends well with the rhythm guitar. The outro features more wild lead guitar as it heads to a final chord.

The song became a mainstay of the live set, where it took on extra life. Australia also got it as a single release (backed with 'Rocker').

'Rocker'

A full-on, almost breathless 'rocker' that became an even more energetic live staple. It's a headlong rush of a song that utilises some pure Little Richard tropes, such as at 0:24, where Bon's delivery is broken by the guitar. That's exactly the kind of thing Little Richard would do. It gives the song a real vintage rock 'n' roll feel, right down to Bon's 'blue suede shoes'. What also contributes to the effect are Angus' wild solos. When it crashes out at 1:50, you believe that's it – all over. But no, back they come in again for what is basically a jam around the main riff. It's a glorious rocker!

'Can I Sit Next To You Girl' (Angus Young/ Malcolm Young)

A tighter and more powerful version of the song than on their debut single. If you didn't know otherwise, you would have said Bon wrote the lyrics, so it shows how in tune the Youngs already were with his style. Okay, it lacks Bon's touches, especially on the very basic chorus, but fundamentally, it doesn't stand out as too different from his style.

The Chuck Berry rhythm stands out a mile, as does the lead line that 'wanders' around it. The drop-down on the chorus, as Bon gets up close and personal, is great; his delivery is pure lechery. Angus adds some howls of lead guitar as things get more excitable. His best part is the flurry of notes he unleashes in the outro. The song might have been improved with more lead guitar.

'High Voltage'

It was released as the first single from the album in June 1975. It was George Young's idea for them to write a song using an A-C-D-C chord sequence. They don't, in fact, quite manage it, with the final chord being another A. Angus told *Guitar World* in July 2008 that, amazingly, the recording was 'the first take we'd done, and every take after that just seemed shallow in comparison. So, that was a first-timer, guitar solo and everything'. It's the song Tony Currenti picks out from his session work because 'every time I play 'High Voltage' with any tribute band, the people stand up. I am very proud of it'. It is indeed a big fan favourite and is a celebratory song of the band in many ways. Bon's lyrics are a 'defence' of his lifestyle and he has no regrets or qualms about it. He has become the 'rock 'n' roll singer'.

Malcolm told *Guitar World* in July 2008 that his only regret was that he couldn't use his 1963 Gretsch Jet Firebird: 'My guitar had been broken, and we had to get the song down that night, so I just grabbed whatever was lying around the studio. I believe it was a Gibson L-5. To this day, I still hear that track and go, 'Ugh'. But other than that, it's the Gretsch on everything'. An interesting facet of the song is George Young's melodic bass playing. Mark

Evans (in his autobiography) described George's playing as 'loopy' and that's a fair assessment. It's as much about the melody as the rhythm. Angus's high lead lick is catchy and Bon, as ever, is so adept at creating the spaces in his vocals to let the band shine through. Currenti plays along with Malcolm on the rhythm, giving George the freedom to play a glorious bass melody line while Angus solos over the top. It's wonderful stuff!

The chorus is so simple yet effective. Angus drops down into a similar rhythm part to Malcolm, which doubles the power. At 1:28, there are some overdubbed castanets by George. You can hear him more clearly still playing them in the chorus at 2:04. Angus gets a short solo before the brief breakdown part, which comes in at 2:48. From there, it's an exultant rush to the end, amusingly with the flattest low-key backing vocals ever. 'High Voltage' is one of the biggest AC/DC songs. It completely sums up their approach.

'School Days' (Chuck Berry)

Despite the Wikipedia entry, Tony Currenti confirms that 'No, I didn't do 'Schooldays''. It was the second and final cover by the band. It wouldn't get an international release until it appeared on the *Volts* disc of *Bonfire*. They treat it with full respect to Berry's original. Fans of a certain age will recognise the roots of early 70s Status Quo here, too! The 'live' feel of the song is part of the charm. Mark's early bass warm-up is kept, as is the band conversation just before they launch into what is the 'keeper take'. The stereo separation is wide, which gives it a more expansive feel rather than mono or tightly panned stereo. Angus and Malcolm are wide apart on each speaker. Malcolm comes in first, followed by Angus's higher counterpoint melody.

Angus's first solo blends in with the rhythm track. He builds from a series of staccato notes to controlled string bends. His second solo (3:45) is even more impressive, after which it's back to the riff till the outro, with the tempo increasing. A good way to finish but not a great one because the song is so close to being an exact cover.

What Happened Next?

AC/DC had their sights initially on the UK as their next goal. Michael Browning's clever promo device was instrumental in getting a deal with Atlantic Records:

> When I was manager for Billy Thorpe & The Aztecs, I got them a deal with RAK Records. I had a machine made by a company called Fairchild. It was a briefcase, and when you opened it, a screen would pop up. You could put your music videos or film clips on the machine and see the band playing live. So, that machine helped me get the deal for Billy Thorpe. I had left the machine in London with my sister Coral. She worked for a company which managed an American keyboard player – John 'Rabbit' Bundrick. Atlantic

wanted him to play with Paul Kossoff's band Back Street Crawler. So she was asked to come into Atlantic to discuss that deal and she took my machine. In the meantime, I made a video of AC/DC in Australia and sent it over to her. The video was great and made the band look huge. Anyway, she pulled out the video in her meeting with Phil Carson at Atlantic and said, 'I want you to see my little brother's band'. She put it on and Carson, after about 30 seconds, said, 'Stop the video!' She thought he didn't like it, but he loved it! Carson said: 'Get him on the phone now!' And that's how it happened with Atlantic. A little while later, we did the deal.

Browning and the band signed with Atlantic via Phil Carson in 1975. Carson was an Executive Vice-President at Atlantic, with responsibilities for the non-American markets. He loved the band so much that he signed them to a 15-album deal, which was phenomenal for a newly signed band. It showed his belief in them but also his shrewdness; he had them committed to one album a year minimum, with an upfront payment of $25,000 per album. Browning adds that 'part of the deal was that the advance would have to be put into bringing the band over to England and having them reside and base themselves there. It meant Atlantic would have them available to do promo, tours, TV shows and so on in the UK and in Europe'.

High Voltage (1976)

Personnel: See previous albums
Produced by Harry Vanda and George Young
Release date: 30 April 1976
Label: Atlantic
Highest chart places: Australia: 13, UK: did not chart, US: 146
Running time: 44:23
All songs by Angus Young, Malcolm Young and Bon Scott
Tracklisting: 'It's A Long Way To The Top', 'Rock 'N' Roll Singer', 'The Jack', 'Live Wire', 'T.N.T.', 'Can I Sit Next To You Girl', 'Little Lover', 'She's Got Balls', 'High Voltage'

Phil Carson picked the tracks from the first two Australian albums for this debut international release. It is still regarded by many as their 'real' debut, with the prior two Australian releases as provincial curios. Carson clearly felt the quality of material had improved by the time of *T.N.T.*, as he only picked 'Little Lover' and 'She's Got Balls' from their debut. Why 'Soul Stripper' wasn't picked is a mystery. Space was partly a problem for track selection, which explains why 'It's A Long Way To The Top' is 12 seconds shorter than it was on *T.N.T.*. The running order could have been improved. 'Live Wire', for instance, just isn't an end-of-side-one track; it's an opening number.

The original European front cover was a poor effort, a lurid, flashy cartoon in a riot of colour. Browning says the band were never too bothered by the international variations of their albums, but this cover was an exception for them. 'There was only one thing that really pissed them off. Atlantic put out the combination album from *High Voltage* and *T.N.T.* and created this horrid pink cover. We saw it and went, 'Who authorised this?' It wasn't me and I still don't know to this day who authorised it. We were all totally bummed out about it, but we got over it'.

The second edition cover is the more familiar and most used one. It's a drawing of Angus, with a guitar, looking straight into the camera with his tongue out. A lightning bolt is either striking or coming out of his right sneaker. The palette is a subdued yellow/brown, but the effect is good enough. Where both covers work extremely well is on the back; they both feature the same superb design of pictures of the band, along with letters sent to them, largely about their behaviour. In the case of Mark Evans, it is based on fact.

High Voltage did a great job as an international introduction to the band, but *T.N.T.* on its own could have done that equally as well if it had been re-packaged.

What Happened Next?

With the support of the London offices of Atlantic Records, the band moved to the UK. It made sense because the market was potentially there and the country is a relatively small place to break through in. Britain, mainland Europe and then America was the route to success.

They arrived on 1 April 1976 and set up base at 49 Inverness Terrace, Bayswater, in London. Their next album (*Dirty Deeds*) was already recorded, but, for now, that was kept under wraps as Atlantic set up promotion for the international *High Voltage*. Significantly, Browning managed to turn one piece of misfortune around to their advantage. Time to *Lock Up Your Daughters*! Browning recalls that 'the *Lock Up Your Daughters* tour happened because of Paul Kossoff's death. They were scheduled to go out on the road with Back Street Crawler and Paul had died on the plane over from New York. We had to conjure up a new way of getting the band out there, so we did a deal with *Sounds* magazine'. They agreed to promote the 19-date tour after seeing a film of the band live at Atlantic's London offices. 'It would have been the same video my sister showed Phil Carson', says Browning.

For £1, or 50p with a voucher cut from the magazine, you could see AC/DC live in what were mostly clubs. More dates followed, including some rearranged gigs with Back Street Crawler gigs. They took special note of Crawler's singer Terry Wilson-Slesser. He impressed them and they remembered him when their backs were to the wall in 1980.

In July, Coral Browning found the band the perfect headquarters and base at 23 Lonsdale Road, Barnes, in London. All but Bon moved in there; he was (according to Mark Evans) now living with his girlfriend Margaret 'Silver' Smith at her flat on Gloucester Road, West Kensington.

Dirty Deeds Done Dirt Cheap (1976)

Personnel:
Bon Scott: lead vocals
Angus Young: lead guitar
Malcolm Young: rhythm guitar, backing vocals
Mark Evans: bass (except on 'There's Gonna Be Some Rockin'")
Phil Rudd: drums
George Young; bass on 'There's Gonna Be Some Rockin'", maracas on 'Problem Child' and 'Jailbreak'
Produced by Harry Vanda and George Young at Albert Studios, Sydney, December 1975 and January 1976
Release date: 20 September 1976 (Australia), 12 November 1976 (UK), March 1981 (US)
Label: Albert/Atlantic
Highest chart places: Australia: 5, UK: did not chart, US: 3
Running time: 42:24 (Australian version), 39:59 (International version)
All songs by Angus Young, Malcolm Young and Bon Scott

The album sessions started in December 1975 with the recording of 'Jailbreak' and 'Fling Thing'. The band then returned to Alberts in January to record the rest of the songs. Britain got a teaser for the album when the band played the Reading Festival on 29 August 1976. In the set was 'Jailbreak', which inexplicably was to be left off the UK edition of the album! Another teasing first for the fans came at that same Reading show with the first-ever Angus strip tease. It wasn't planned in advance, as Angus admitted to *Total Guitar* in 2020: 'Some blonde girl walked real slow across the photo pit right in front of the stage and 30,000 eyes went with her. It was a real showstopper. Malcolm said to me, 'You gotta do something to get the crowd's attention back!' So I dropped my trousers'.

Dirty Deeds was supposed to be the start of worldwide synchronicity on AC/DC album releases, but, to Phil Carson's horror, Atlantic USA passed on the album and were about to drop AC/DC. Carson managed to salvage matters and ensured there would be at least one more chance for the band in America. Were Atlantic USA right to pass on *Dirty Deeds*? For the bulk of the album, it's hard to understand why because there are some solid gold AC/DC songs, save for the execrable 'Big Balls'. However, songs such as 'Squealer', 'Love At First Feel' and 'Big Balls' may well have made a few of the powers that be shudder over the lyrics. Mark Evans (in his autobiography) says the label were also unhappy with Bon's vocals and the production. Yet, fundamentally, the album is in the same mould as their previous two and, of course, the international *High Voltage*. The band had delivered similarly again, so Atlantic were maybe hoping for something more refined this time.

Yet the next album, *Let There Be Rock*, was as raw as anything the band ever did. Atlantic USA released that, so you have to presume it was the material on *Dirty Deeds* that they disliked. If, as Mark suggests, Bon's voice was a problem, wouldn't Atlantic have pushed for him to be replaced at this point? Browning says Bon's position was never in doubt, at least with the Youngs: 'Not at all. The band loved Bon; they would never do that. He had his issues, which everyone knows about, but he was always there when he needed to be, writing lyrics when he needed to and there for the gigs when he needed to be. He was reliable and very loveable'. There might have been issues starting with Mark Evans, though. Some have questioned how much he contributes to the album, with suggestions that George Young plays most of the bass.

A bastardised version of the album was eventually released in 1981 by Atlantic US after Doug Morris from the label discovered they had an AC/DC album ready in the vaults, albeit a five-year-old one with a different lead singer!

As well as differences on the Australian and international tracklists (noted below), the covers are completely different interpretations of the evocative title. In Australia, they went with a cartoon front and back cover design by Kettle Art Productions. On the front are Angus and Bon by a pool table, with Bon flashing the title, which is tattooed on his forearm. The other three are on the back cover, with Malcolm holding out a prophetic can of beer.

'The band didn't like the Australian cover', says Browning, 'so we hired Hipgnosis for the international cover. They came up with the concept of all those people standing in front of a hotel'. It was a sign of the band's growing status that in-vogue sleeve designers Hipgnosis got the contract to come up with a sleeve. They were arguably the number one album sleeve design company of the time – so not cheap. Browning asserts that it wasn't, as has been claimed elsewhere, a rejected design that was going to be used for another band. This was the most lavish package yet, with a cover full of mystery and menace. It's actually a montage, with the motel backdrop photographed separately from the foreground people. As was often usual with Hipgnosis, there are no band pictures until you get to the inner sleeve. Here, the lyrics are interspersed with band shots (taken in the dressing room of The Marquee in London), with the same black banner over their eyes as the figures on the outer sleeve.

'Dirty Deeds Done Dirt Cheap'

This was inspired by an American animated children's TV series called *Beany And Cecil*. 'It was a cartoon when I was a kid', Angus recalled to *Guitar World* in 2009. 'There's a character in it called Dishonest John. He used to carry this card with 'Dirty Deeds Done Dirt Cheap – Special Rates, Holidays' written on it. I stored up a lot of these things in my brain'. It's a great opening track and proved to be even better live, where it gained that extra spark to make it an undoubted AC/DC classic. That rising chorus, with the audience joining in, is just magic.

The killer opening guitar riff carries the right amount of menace. There is a taut, restrained feel to it as well, adding to the sense of threat. The background panting is a nice touch, too, though what it's supposed to represent as a 'dirty deed' is anybody's guess! Phil's fill and cymbal crash at the end of each verse is a nice switch into the chorus. You have to love the gang vocals singing the last part of the title with audible relish! Angus's solo features the fast, fluid notes (at 2:15) that he would later refine for the riff of 'Thunderstruck'. There's a nervy edge to the notes he plays, contributing to the drama. The finale is a blasting wall of noise, as Bon lists his available dirty deeds, including 'High Voltage'!

The phone number that Bon gives is the highly memorable 36-24-36! When the album was eventually released in America, the number became a problem for Norman and Marilyn White from Libertyville, Illinois. Fans who misheard Bon's 'hey' as 'eight' rang 3624368, which was the Whites' number. Annoyed by the relentless phone calls, the Whites sued the band for $250,000 in damages, demanding that the song be altered. Fortunately, the judge threw the case out.

The song was released as a single in Australia, backed with 'R.I.P. (Rock In Peace)'.

'Ain't No Fun (Waiting 'Round To Be A Millionaire)'

There are some familiar elements of AC/DC on this one. The intro nods, in part, towards 'You Shook Me All Night Long', while the main riff is firmly out of the 'It's A Long Way To The Top' territory. The link-up between Angus and Malcolm on the riff is great, with Angus adding a catchy element around Malcolm's more simple and direct approach. The preamble by Bon, detailing that it's a true story and 'only the names have been changed to protect the innocent', could probably apply to a fair few of his lyrics! The chorus showcases the potential they would explore later on: a big sound with ringing guitars, the only thing missing being strong backing vocals. It's an astonishingly long track (at 6:57), given how little there is to it. What they do is split it into two halves: The first half is in a slow/mid-tempo based around the riff, and then, at 3:51, they pick up the tempo for what is basically a faster take on the song. It's a neat trick and the song works just as well, if not better, at the higher tempo. Phil's drumming is more forceful and prominent in the second half.

It's a good song, but it could have been better if it had been developed more. The riff and the energy level keep your attention, though.

'There's Gonna Be Some Rockin''

Mark recalls (in *Dirty Deeds*) that it was George Young who got the songwriting process going by playing a shuffle rhythm on the bass. At the heart of AC/DC is the 12-bar blues, which is where the similarities, at times, to Status Quo come from. This has a warm, mid-tempo boogie feel to it that works well. It also sounds like a live recording; such is the feel of it. That's George on bass and the fact he plays on such a simple track instead of Mark Evans, kind of adds fuel to the suspicions he also might be on the more challenging songs.

Lyrically, it's very basic, but it's a fair summary of the band's live ambitions. Angus's solos are very much in a Chuck Berry style that fits the song well. The occasional use of stop-start vocal motifs is another homage back to the tropes found in 1950s rockers. While this is by no means a great song, there's enough about it to stand repeated listening.

'Problem Child'

Angus revealed to *Total Guitar* in 2020 that, 'He (Bon) did say he wrote 'Problem Child' for me, but, you know, I never owned a knife like it says in the song. My dad took my knife off me when I was four. Just having a guitar was bad enough, I suppose. But yeah, Bon summed me up in two words!'

It's a classic AC/DC song that sums up everything that makes them great. It opens with that precision, catchy, blasting riff from Malcolm. Bon comes in with a dismissive 'Cop this' at the 14-second mark. At this point, there's only him, Malcolm and Phil in the song. Mark Evans comes in at around 0:30, while Angus isn't present until 1:49, unless he is doubling Malcolm's riff before that. His big entrance comes at 1:49 with a solo that sits in well with the riff and ups the energy levels.

Next, there's a bit of George Young magic at work. As they return to the riff at 2:27, he overdubs maracas, which adds to the rhythm. Angus's second solo comes in at 2:37 and is initially similar in approach to his earlier one, accompanied by gang shouts of the title. As Angus persists, he builds the solo until it becomes all-encompassing right through to the outro, with those maracas still intact! The piercing trilling notes Angus gets in from 4:30 are superb, giving the song a dramatic ending. The crescendo ending is one of their best, followed by a cheeky coda of the main riff (plus maracas) coming briefly back in.

Atlantic knew the song was special, too, because it was resurrected, albeit edited without the coda, for *Let There Be Rock*.

'Squealer'

This raunchy rocker is a real tour de force musically, and Bon's vocal delivery is full of well-judged inflections. If there is a problem, it's with the lyrics, which are uneasy at best. Bon's conspiratorial, hushed, but lecherous tone in the first part of the song adds to the effect.

The bass riff grabs your attention, melodic and powerful, sounding a lot like George Young at work. Verging on a soul/funk style, the track harks back to 'Soul Stripper'. Malcolm's jagged riff at 1:38 gears things up just as Bon switches to a more full-on delivery. The chorus sees Malcolm (and somebody else) intoning the title, with Bon adding the licentious details. The solo at

45

2:37 is great, but if it sounds familiar, it's because it's the same solo that appears in 'Dirty Deeds' at 2:00. Angus keeps going all the way to the outro for what is a dynamic and thrilling end to the song.

'Big Balls'

Bon adopting the voice of a gin-soaked upper-class toff is amusing for a bit, as is the comical guitar riff that opens it. But, overall, this song is a pun that wears thin quickly and should have been rejected. It's puerile nonsense, and musically, it's not up to much either, sounding little better than a studio rehearsal. It really is all about the lyrics. Ideally, this would have been better left as a B-side (at best) and 'Love At First Feel' included instead as a much better alternative.

'R.I.P. (Rock In Peace)'

This was not included on the international edition. That decision was surely because the song's riff and melody are so close to 'There's Gonna Be Some Rockin''. This, though, is marginally the better song of the two; it's a tad more energetic and has more interesting lyrics. Bon amusingly gives away the song's antecedents in the final outro verse, where he name-checks Chuck Berry, Little Richard and Jerry Lee Lewis. It's Chuck who has the most influence, as the song is firmly in 12-bar blues/ Chuck Berry territory. The gang vocals in the chorus add to the good-time feel that shines through. Somehow, they manage to stretch the song out to 3:36, which is longer than it deserves to be. It appeared as the B-side to 'Dirty Deeds' in Australia, but it didn't get an international release until it was rounded up for the *Backtracks* box set.

'Ride On'

A song that got overlooked at the time. Its presence on the *Who Made Who* soundtrack saw it receive wider listening and critical acclaim, and it has become something of a personal eulogy by and for Bon Scott. It has a blues feel, which they might have explored more on their albums. It's clever how they stick to the laid-back blues. There are times when you think it will explode into something else, but instead, they pull it back. It does build up to a peak in the outro when the tempo rises after a fill from Malcolm. Angus tastefully solos over the outro and gets the final notes to himself. The song still surprises you with the brooding intensity. Bon's vocal is particularly well phrased and expressed. It's easily one of his best performances with the band.

'Jailbreak'

A stunning finish to the album. It's one of the best songs from the Bon Scott era and deserved better than to have stuttered out internationally later on the *74 Jailbreak* release. It was released as a single on 14 June in the UK, which was likely why it was 'dropped' from the international edition of the album.

It opens with the slashing guitar riff, akin to 'It's A Long Way To The Top'. It also shares an irresistible groove, featuring a swinging bass line, and maracas, courtesy of George. The riff and Bon's tour-de-force vocal give this song a hard edge. This is a much grittier version of a jailbreak than McCartney's 'Band On The Run'! The escape itself has heartbeat bass, followed by guitar sound effects from Angus, who swoops for the spotlights, blasts out the sirens and, finally, incorporates stuttering notes for the rifles that conclusively hit Bon. He audibly grimaces in pain 'with a bullet in his back'. It's back to the joyous swinging groove after that, with surprisingly subtle lead licks from Angus. He doesn't smash it in the way you might expect.

The video for the song was shot in a quarry in the Sunshine suburb of Melbourne.

International Edition

'Rock In Peace' and 'Jailbreak' were removed and replaced in what was also a different running order. How 'Big Balls' passed quality control is a mystery, but there you go!

The new sequence ran as follows: 'Dirty Deeds Done Dirt Cheap', 'Love At First Feel', 'Big Balls', 'Rocker', 'Problem Child', 'There's Gonna Be Some Rockin'', 'Ain't No Fun (Waiting Round To Be A Millionaire)', 'Ride On', 'Squealer'. The two new tracks are 'Rocker', salvaged from the Australian *T.N.T*, having not already been re-used for *High Voltage* (international edition), and the entirely new 'Love At First Feel'. 'Dirty Deeds' is edited (21 seconds shorter) to keep the album length down, as is 'Rocker' (six seconds shorter).

'Love At First Feel'

It was added to side one of the album. In the verses, it is musically similar in its melody to 'High Voltage'. It's another one rooted in the band's love of Chuck Berry. The chorus is solid, resting on Malcolm's crunching guitar, the rock-steady rhythm section and the full-on gang vocals. Angus's terrific solo (1:35), with a series of howling licks, is layered over the backing track shuffle rhythm. As he finishes off, the backing track drops down to Phil alone, as he cues the gang vocals back in. It's a delightful small touch, with the song then building back up as Bon comes back in.

This is one of those forgotten songs that deserves more exposure and re-evaluation. Australia also got it as a non-album single backed with 'Problem Child', making for a great 7' release.

Related Track:
'Fling Thing'

This brief (mostly) instrumental was released as the B-side to 'Jailbreak'. The original song it is based on started out as a poem, written by Andrew Lang in 1876, called 'The Bonnie Banks O' Loch Lomond'. It's a live-in-the-studio recording and a little light relief for the band. Towards the end, Bon ad-libs in a Scottish brogue and we then get a tantalising snatch of lead guitar and the riff from Little Richard's 'Lucille'. A nice bit of fun, but it should never have even been a B-side.

The 1976 European Sessions

AC/DC recorded at two studios in September. The first was Vineyard Studios in London, where the intent was to record an EP. They recorded at least the following tracks: 'Carry Me Home', 'Cold Hearted Man', 'Dirty Eyes' and 'Love At First Feel'. While the EP was abandoned, the four songs have all subsequently appeared on albums/CDs. 'Cold Hearted Man' is reviewed under *Powerage,* where it initially made the tracklist, while 'Love At First Feel' is reviewed under *Dirty Deeds,* as it was added to the international version.

The second session was a short notice one in Maschen, Germany, to record 'I'm A Rebel'. These five recordings are the only ones Mark Evans made with the band outside Australia.

'Carry Me Home'

This was released first as the B-side to 'Dog Eat Dog' and then as a 'rarity' on the *Backtracks* box set. It's a good enough song, with a loose feel to it mirroring the subject matter. Bon sings about a night on the town, amusingly becoming progressively more slurred as it goes on.

'Dirty Eyes'

This was first released on *Bonfire.* The music was re-used for 'Whole Lotta Rosie', and in this version, it has a looser, less staccato feel to it, which, in its way, works well. The chorus is less effective than 'Rosie', not reaching anywhere near the same peak. Equally, the lyrics are no match for 'Rosie' either. However, if this was an outtake, and there was no 'Rosie' to compare it to, it would be hailed as a hidden gem. It's well worth a listen.

'I'm A Rebel' (Alex Young)

This was written by their older brother. Malcolm Dome and Jerry Ewing (in *The AC/DC Encyclopedia*) claim the session was on 16 September 1976 at Studio Maschen (in Maschen), which is near Hamburg. AC/DC played Hamburg on 15 September and Studio Maschen themselves confirmed AC/DC recorded there on their website, listing them as one of their clients.

Allegedly, the promoter Rudy Holzhauer asked the band to record Alex's song. The session supposedly featured the band, plus Alex Young on lead vocals. Bon sang backing vocals and played drums (so maybe Phil didn't contribute at all). Whether AC/DC had thoughts of recording it properly or whether they were merely acting as a backing band on Alex Young's demo is open to conjecture. In 1979, producer Dirk Steffens, who knew Alex Young, asked him if he had anything that could get the German heavy metal band Accept a hit. They gratefully used this catchy rock song as the title track of their 1980 album.

Let There Be Rock (1977)

Personnel:
Bon Scott: lead vocals
Angus Young: lead guitar
Malcolm Young: rhythm guitar, backing vocals
Mark Evans: bass
Phil Rudd: drums
Produced by Harry Vanda and George Young at Albert Studios, Sydney, January – February 1977
Release date: 21 March 1977 (Australia), 25 July 1977 (International)
Label: Albert/Atlantic
Highest chart places: Australia: 19, UK: 17, USA: 154
Running time: 40:19 (Australian version), 41:01 (International version)
All songs by Angus Young, Malcolm Young and Bon Scott, except as noted

While it was their first original album to be released in all markets in the same year, the synchronicity didn't extend to either the tracklist or the cover. It is, however, a classic AC/DC album. Angus recalled to *Guitar World* in 2000 that 'of all the many albums we'd done with my brother George and his partner Harry Vanda, the one Mutt (Lange) wished he would have done, where he was envious of George, was *Let There Be Rock*'. The mind boggles to think what Lange would have brought to the album!

Mark Evans, speaking to *Rocktopia* in 2012, felt it was an important album because:

I could put my finger on the timeline and say, *Let There Be Rock*; that's where the band started. It sounded like AC/DC before, of course, with *T.N.T.* and *Dirty Deeds*, but that's where they stuck the whole thing down to a fine point. They'd lost a little bit of that whimsical sort of thing. One of the things I love about AC/DC is there's a sense of humour to it. With Bon's stuff, there was a sharp sense of humour. It was just funny stuff, very witty and great lyrics.

Angus went even further in praising the album. When Swiss radio station SRF 3 asked him, in 2020, which album he would play to impress a first-time listener, he didn't hesitate: '*Let There Be Rock*, for me, is the album'. He went on to recall the game plan for the album: 'George asked me and Malcolm, 'What sort of album do you wanna do this time?' And Malcolm just looked at me and he said, 'We just want an album that's just gonna be pure hard rock guitar'.' And in a little over two weeks, that is exactly what they came up with.

It is, in effect, a two-fingers up to Atlantic from a band who were still angry at the non-release of *Dirty Deeds* in America. You can hear the seething potent rage that permeates the record right from the opening notes of 'Go Down'. That continues with barely any let-up, especially on the international version, with 'Problem Child' adding to the ferocity instead of the left-field detour of 'Crabsody In Blue'.

The Australian cover is a wonderful gatefold grey-scale design package. The front cover is a close-up of blurred fingers flying along a fretboard. As Angus and Malcolm were unavailable, photographer Colin Stead got Colin Turner (guitarist with Australian band Buffalo) to pose for the shots. The inner gatefold features excellent live shots of the band, and in truth, one of these would have made an even better front cover. The Australian edition was released just two days after the cover photos for the International were taken. It suggests the possibility that the Australian cover design was used quickly out of necessity.

The international cover marks the first appearance of Gerard Huerta's iconic logo. Keith Morris took the cover photographs at the Kursaal Ballroom, Southend, on 19 March 1977. The front cover is curiously static and all but Angus are in shadows or obscured. The Biblical light from above is apt, but there is a lot of empty space around it. It could have been much a much better design. Worse still is the rushed-looking back cover, a close-up of Angus riffing away. It's a great shot, yes, but one of each member of the band would surely have been better.

The album itself is a great one, nonetheless. The quality is reflected in the live setlists over the decades where 'Let There Be Rock', 'Bad Boy Boogie', 'Hell Ain't A Bad Place To Be' and 'Whole Lotta Rosie', as well as several other songs, became firm favourites.

'Go Down'

This is a great, no-nonsense opening song. A real statement of intent. Bon leaves us in no doubt as to who exactly is 'going down'. It's Ruby (Lips) in the first half and she is no lift attendant! She was apparently a groupie, her real name allegedly Wendy, from Melbourne. The more mysterious Mary takes over for the second half and also seems to have a particular set of skills!

It's monstrously heavy from the off, with a real swing to it. A key part of that swing comes when Angus plays his ecstatic or teasing fills over the crunching rhythm. The chorus takes things up several notches with strong backing vocals, though less harmonious than they will be later under Mutt Lange. Angus's solo is quite lyrical and leads into a bridge section at 3:23, where the band take it down. It's a great part, with a soft shuffle from the rhythm section and tasty blues licks from Angus emphasising Bon's 'situation'. As Bon gets more excited, the band head for the climax.

Quirkily, the song faded out on the original vinyl and CD issues, but it has been corrected for the remasters series and now ends with the big finish the song should have always had.

'Dog Eat Dog'

The trials and tribulations of the music world form the basis of the subject matter here. Band manager Michael Browning aptly used it as the title of his book.

This is a gritty track driven along by a jabbing guitar riff and relatively busy drums from Phil. Bon gets real venom and anger into his vocals, the only consolation being that 'every dog has his day'. The guitar solo, by contrast, is quite restrained, and what sounds like a lively lick from Angus doesn't get the prominence it deserves on the outro because of the dense production. This is a good track, which was picked out as a single in Australia. Not an easy choice for Alberts; there were better songs to pick, but it did have the non-album 'Carry Me Home' on the B-side.

'Let There Be Rock'

A classic 'creation of rock 'n' roll' song that defines Bon Scott era AC/DC. This would also be a contender for the song that best sums up what Malcolm adds to the sound. He simply powers this along in what is a frantic assault from the band. The rhythm section are at their most intense here. Famously, they recorded four takes of the backing tracks and it was take two that was deemed the keeper. Any thoughts of a rest between takes for Phil were put aside because he had no qualms about repeating the punishing rhythm without losing the beat.

After the thunderous intro, the backing track drops to just Mark and Phil for the first verse, with Malcolm coming back in with a sawing riff after Bon exclaims, 'Let there be rock'. Angus soon joins in with a harmony riff and the first of his lead parts. The signature lick he plays at 1:43 closes his solo and heralds the return of that intro riff and rhythm. For the second verse – 'And it came to pass' – it drops down again to Bon, Mark and Phil. Again, Bon cues the guitars back in and Angus gets another lead part, for which he plays some 50s-style rock 'n' roll licks over Malcolm's chopping rhythm. Angus finishes off again with that signature lick. For the third and final verse – 'One night in a club called the Shakin' Hand' – the guitars come in for a response to Bon and it sets the song up for the final blast all the way to the outro and that famous solo from Angus, which he finished with smoke billowing out of his amp!

It was released as a single, backed with 'Problem Child', but it was too full-on for UK radio, and even their loyal Australian fans only got it to number 82. Onstage, the song found extra legs, becoming an elongated extravaganza.

'Bad Boy Boogie'

This was one of the first songs that came together for the album. Listen carefully in the intro and you can hear the tape machine winding up to maximum speed while Phil sorts out his hi-hat. It's all about that immense, powerful riff and Bon outlining just how bad he can be. At 2:04, a heavier doubled (new) riff comes in, which leads up to Angus's solo. Angus gets to tear it up over the intense backing rhythm track, but the best is yet to come. At 2:47, right after the solo, Angus plays a droning lead part over the crashing rhythm track. It's a brilliant detour which leads back into the main riff again, with Bon sounding more euphoric than ever.

This classic song was extended on stage, where it also featured Angus's strip-tease.

'Overdose'

It opens with almost tentative arpeggios from Angus before settling into the riff and a blistering, full-on performance. Credit here to Mark, whose bass work is a perfect metronomic pulse, and then there's the rolling rhythmic groove from Malcolm. Angus gets off some great lead parts, delving into the blues runs he so often uses. You can hear the intro of what will be 'Rock 'N' Roll Damnation' in his guitar fills. This song is unjustly often overlooked, overshadowed by the bigger songs on the album, which got more live traction.

'Crabsody In Blue'

Malcolm explained how the song came about to *Guitar World* in July 2008: 'We all got the crabs at one time or another. They would spread in the car! We were touring in Australia at the time, and in just about every town we went to, somebody had to go into the VD clinic. Crabs and scabies were rampant at the time. Because every band were screwing the same women'.

This, obviously, was the controversial track on the album as far as Atlantic were concerned. But even if you ignore their concerns, the bigger issue is that this is the weakest song on the album and filler at best. It's in the same ballpark as 'The Jack', both in subject matter and musically, for which they opt appropriately to play the blues. There's little special about it other than Angus's burning solo. 'Cold Hearted Man' would have been a better choice here as an unused (at that time) track.

'Hell Ain't A Bad Place To Be'

The tuning is noticeably off on the guitars. George Young decided to go with it because he felt the vibe was right. To a degree, he was correct because this is authentic and in your face, but I would still take the live version on *If You Want Blood* over this any day. Compare Bon's intro 'Hey you', for example. He sounds almost polite here, compared to the more demonstrative instruction on *If You Want Blood*. It's still a great song, though, bound to one of their most best and most effective riffs, with a masterful vocal from Bon (save for that intro). The guy definitely had a way of putting across the lyrics and making them sound personal and meaningful.

'Whole Lotta Rosie'

The song is 'about' Bon's night of passion with a lady whom he estimated was about six-foot-two, weighed 305 pounds and had measurements, as featured in the lyrics, of '42-39-56'. Angus recalled the story to *Guitar World* in 2000:

We were playing in Tasmania (likely Hobart on 7 January 1977). Bon had gone out one night after we'd been playing. He'd just been wandering the streets around the little club areas. And he was walking past this street and this girl grabbed him from a doorway. She pulled him in and said, 'Hey, Bon, in here'. And he thought, 'Hey, why not?' The girl was there with her girlfriend, and he spent the night. This girl who was with Bon was a fair-sized girl. She said, 'Bon, these last few months I've been with 28 famous people'. And she was giving him the low-down of politicians and different people she'd been out with and whatever. Anyhow, the next morning, Bon woke up sort of pinned to the wall. The girl thought Bon was still sleeping. She leaned across to her girlfriend, who was sharing the room, and she said, 'twenty-nine'. Her name being Rosie, Bon thought it was a great title for a song. He said this girl was worthy of being put into a piece of poetry.

AC/DC biographer Jesse Fink offers a credible story on his website that the lady concerned was the late Rose-Maree Caroll. The music was originally for a song they were working on called 'Dirty Eyes'. Bon replaced the lyrics after he was 'inspired' by Rosie! Another inspiration is in the title itself, a reference to Led Zeppelin's 'Whole Lotta Love'. The song captures an old-school Little Richard feel in the delivery. This is very much a high-octane rock 'n' roll song once it gets going. It opens with Malcolm's syncopated guitar riff and Phil's drums. Bon is quite understated in the first verse till his final cry of 'you could say she got it all', which cues the deadly full tempo riff and rhythm. The riff is stunning, coming at you with unstoppable force. While the choruses are great, it's that riff and the movement on the verses that is the killer part of the song. Angus's first solo (2:20) is a cracker, but he tops even that with his second one. The stop/start riff interplay at 2:50 between Angus and Malcolm is the cue. Angus picks up on the riff and soars off, his fingers flying over the fretboard till Bon comes back in, accompanied (if you listen carefully) by a wolf-whistle kiss-off from Angus. Angus gets in a third solo with over a minute to go but keeps your attention to the end. That third solo is easily up there in his personal best list.

The song itself is deservedly one of the biggest and best in the AC/DC catalogue. It was released as a single (backed with 'Dog Eat Dog') and was their first UK charting single, reaching number 68. The Netherlands loved it even more and sent it to number five.

International Variation
'Problem Child' was substituted for 'Crabsody In Blue' and opened side two instead of 'Overdose', which dropped down to being the second song on that side. It's the same song as was featured on *Dirty Deeds* but without the reprise coda.

What Happened Next?
Mark Evans was fired by the band in May 1977 following the first European leg of the *Let There Be Rock* world tour. There were, it seems, some differences between him and Angus. Browning explains that:

There were some personal issues, but I think it was a combination of that and playing. I think they wanted someone who could be a better player. It was compounded by the fact that Angus, Malcolm and Bon are all of Scottish descent and there was always a bit of that 'you're not part of the family of Scots', you know? Anyone coming into that band who wasn't Scottish was never really going to get to the core of everything.

Mark Evans stated in his autobiography that, at a meeting with the band and Michael Browning, Malcolm told him that they wanted a bass player who could sing backups. From his account, it seems clear that the driving forces behind the decision were Malcolm and Angus. It seems, surprisingly, that they didn't have a replacement already in mind. Edinburgh-born Ian Hampton had been playing sessions since leaving Sparks in early 1976 and he seemed to have the right credentials:

They weren't happy with the bass player they had. I don't remember who put me onto them, but it was somebody in the business. We (Bon and I) got on so well. But, then again, I would probably be long-dead if I had joined them. Bon and I used to go crazy on the booze! I rehearsed with them for a whole week in Battersea; I drove Bon back to his flat in Bayswater every night after rehearsals. I would have a couple of drinks with him, but then the drugs came out and I had to leave.

Hampton, it seemed, fitted the bill: 'Angus and Malcolm wanted me, but Phil Rudd hated me because he loved their bass player. Anyway, I got offered the gig. Then I got talked out of joining'. Hampton says a friend and former P.A. told him: 'Do you really want to spend the rest of your life in a band with a guitarist who wears shorts and a schoolboy uniform? Why don't you come to America and work with Elizabeth Barraclough?' So, I took that option – big mistake'.

Another nearly man was Colin Pattenden from Manfred Mann's Earth Band, suggested by Browning. Malcolm had seen Pattenden play with the band at a one-day festival at Sydney's Randwick Racecourse on 9 May 1971. The other big bands appearing were Free and Deep Purple, but Malcolm was taken with Pattenden's bass playing, which worked so well in tandem with the band's drummer Chris Slade. Pattenden didn't quite fit what they wanted, but Slade's time with AC/DC would come later on.

The man who got the gig was Cliff Williams (born 14 December 1949, Romford). Cliff had previously been the bassist with Home, who also featured future Wishbone Ash guitarist Laurie Wisefield. Cliff recalled his audition to Metal Hammer in 2005: 'I had an audition in Pimlico in a tiny room. The first tracks I played with them were 'Live Wire', 'Problem Child' and, if I remember, some blues. The manager told me afterwards I had the job'. Cliff was officially appointed in June 1977.

There was another personnel issue in 1977. Bon disclosed in a letter to one Valerie Lary (dated August 1977, Pittsburgh) that there had been problems with Phil Rudd. 'Phil had a bit of a nervous breakdown and had to spend a lot of time with a shrink. It was really bad, but luckily, he got over it quickly enough not to upset the band. We had to treat him with kid gloves for a bit, but he's okay now'. With Phil in better shape and Cliff in the band, AC/DC set off to record in Sydney.

The 1977 Sydney Sessions

The band recorded at Alberts Studios in early July 1977. Four of the songs from these sessions were 'Kicked In The Teeth', 'Up To My Neck In You', 'What's Next To The Moon' and the early version of 'Touch Too Much'. The first three were re-recorded for *Powerage*, but the latter only emerged on the *Volts* CD included in the *Bonfire* box set.

'Touch Too Much'

It has little in common with the *Highway To Hell* track except for the title and a similar feel in the melodies, which are played at a higher tempo. The chorus is really strong, and overall, this is a worthwhile outtake that stands up well in its own right. A real gem of a song.

What Happened Next?

AC/DC commenced their first-ever American tour on 27 July 1977 with a show supporting Moxy at the Armadillo World Headquarters in Austin, Texas. The British dates saw a surprise concert that speedily enhanced their breakthrough there. After a two-night stand at Hammersmith Odeon on 25/26 October, they had booked a day off to relax, moving a planned gig at Great Yarmouth from 27 October to 3 November. However, The Sensational Alex Harvey Band (SAHB) pulled out of a gig at Golder's Green Hippodrome to be filmed and shown as part of the BBC's *Sight And Sound In Concert* TV show. AC/DC were in town and available, so they accepted the offered appearance. They absolutely smashed it with a superb, barnstorming performance. The TV coverage (shown on Saturday, 29 October) was priceless and a real talking point. AC/DC gained at SAHB's expense. They had shared roots and principles, but AC/DC were going up while SAHB were coming down.

Powerage (1978)

Personnel:
Bon Scott: lead vocals
Angus Young: lead guitar
Malcolm Young: rhythm guitar, backing vocals
Cliff Williams: bass, backing vocals
Phil Rudd: drums
George Young: maracas and tambourine on 'Rock 'N' Roll Damnation'
Mark Evans: bass on 'Cold Hearted Man'
Produced by Harry Vanda and George Young at Albert Studios, Sydney, February
– March 1978
Release date: 5 May 1978 (Australia/UK), 30 May 1978 (USA)
Label: Albert/Atlantic
Highest chart places: Australia: 22, UK: 26, USA: 133
Running time: 39:47
All songs by Angus Young, Malcolm Young and Bon Scott

There was an intention for musical changes on this album. Angus reflected
to *The Quietus* in 2014 that '*Powerage* was probably us experimenting a little
bit'. That doesn't really ring true; there's still an emphasis on tracks that are
out-and-out rockers, along with 'Gone Shootin'', which stands out as a laid-
back groove. If there is any experimental side to the album, then 'What's Next
To The Moon' would be the primary focus. It's one of the most unusual songs
the band have ever recorded, showcasing a low, muted, stripped-back feel.

Lyrically, *Powerage* is the most 'mainstream' yet from Bon, and he explained
why to the *Liverpool Echo* on 6 May 1978: 'We've had to try and make it
slightly more commercial than our previous albums so that we can get more
airplay'. He's no doubt referring to the music as well as his lyrics.

One obstacle in recording the album was the delay in Cliff getting his visa
to enter Australia. It's odd when you consider he had been there once already
for the 1977 sessions. Yet, grumbled Cliff, in *Metal Hammer* in 2005, 'The
Australian immigration service wasn't good with me'. While waiting for Cliff,
the band kept busy working on the tracks. There are rumours that George
Young actually handled some of the bass parts.

The arrival of Cliff completed the classic AC/DC rhythm section. Phil and
Cliff quickly became a dynamite combination, and with Malcolm's rhythm
guitar on top, they were just unbeatable. There in that threesome's intuitive
understanding lay a big part of AC/DC's enduring success.

The determination to finally break out big meant they spent longer
recording this album than any previous one. In spite of their efforts, the
one thing Atlantic were still concerned about was the lack of a single. Bon's
thoughts about making the album more commercial had not produced the
right song. So the band hurriedly recorded 'Rock 'N' Roll Damnation', which
was a perfect fit.

The album title is fitting and unique; the only reference on the net to 'powerage' is in connection with AC/DC. One wonders if they actually meant it to read 'power age'. It has had a chequered release history, with different tracklists and even mixes. In the CD age, the American tracklist and mix became the one that was used and this has been repeated through the subsequent remasters. For the sake of consistency, on this occasion, the latest remaster, as authorised by the band, is taken as definitive here.

The cover was another first for the band, with the Australian and International versions being the same. Huerta's logo isn't used for this one, with the designer opting to reinforce the title with an 'electric' logo. The image of Angus has been colourised and adapted and has a comic-book feel to it. While it is eye-catching, it doesn't suggest it's an album by a major band – it looks 'cheap'. AC/DC were aiming for the premier league of rock bands and needed everything to be as spot-on as possible. The back cover group shot, taken by Jim Houghton, captures the personalities of the band well. Angus is in the same clothes as he is on the front cover, which is likely an adapted cropped image from another group shot by Houghton.

Powerage is often acclaimed as being the 'best' album from the Bon Scott era. In many ways, it's also a farewell to the band's early years. Bon opined to the *Liverpool Echo* on 6 May 1978 that 'the thing about our music is that no matter what you do, you'll never really change the sound or direction. It's just us playing and enjoying ourselves, which is how it should be'. He also stated that he thought Angus was 'playing better than ever on the new album'. While Bon remained for their next album, it wasn't the same as before. The band evolved with Mutt Lange and entered that premier league of rock bands. Famous fans who swear by it include Slash and Keith Richards, but among those who weren't so convinced were Atlantic Records again. Browning points out that:

There were high expectations from the record label that the group would go to Australia and record an album that would take them to the next level. That didn't really happen. It was a great album; AC/DC fans often say it's their favourite from that era, and it would be my favourite, too. But as a commercial success, it didn't do what the record label wanted it to do; it didn't resonate with the American FM radio stations. The band had built up a pretty solid following with the previous releases and there was an expectation that *Powerage* would break them wide open.

'Rock 'N' Roll Damnation'

At the time, it was noted that the riff to Foreigner's 'Hot Blooded' was out of the same box as this one. It was the obvious single and considerably more commercial than the rest of the album it was bolted onto. Atlantic got their single! In tone and feel, it edges more towards the Mutt Lange era. Vanda and Young used every trick they knew to make the song a hit. There are maracas and a tambourine (care of George Young) added to the driving rhythm track to add colour, a catchy solid riff and a big sing-along chorus.

The mood-setting intro is great: a big crash in and riff with Angus's high melody line. From there, it heads down into the poppy but still heavy riff. It's catchy, too, with those insistent maracas. Bon turns in a defiant, chest-beating vocal, and the only slight flaw is that they don't ramp the backing vocals up more for the chorus. Angus's solo is perhaps more restrained than normal; doubtless, they didn't want to distract from the melodic riff and vocals too much. It may be 'poppy', but it's a great song and the single release signified the band were heading for better times. They got TV exposure with it and the UK sent it to number 24, while the Netherlands placed it higher still at number 18.

'Down Payment Blues'
A deep gem in the back catalogue. Bon's lyrics are a wry look at the continued perilous state of his finances as they awaited the elusive sales and financial rewards. As desperate as things are, Bon cannot resist the amusing payoff line of, 'Can't even feed my cat!' His personality makes the lyrics come to life.

The rhythm section are on fire. Already, it's apparent how well Phil and Cliff work together and this is one of several great examples on the album. Meanwhile, it's Malcolm's guitar that gives the song the character that pushes it up several notches. It's a great riff, too, doubled by the Youngs. Angus's solo, meanwhile, is a killer, summing up the angst in the words with every note. The original release in the UK misses out the final guitar coda and is arguably better for it!

'Gimme A Bullet'
A great intro, with the Youngs fitting together seamlessly. Down in the engine room, Cliff gets to play some almost funky licks at times to break up his runs. It's a catchy song, too, with the twin rhythm guitars giving the track its sting and bite. Bon delivers it well, ranging from a conversational approach to full-on vocals, always sounding completely convincing. Surprisingly, there is no guitar solo in the song, but you don't actually miss it. Maybe they couldn't see where it would fit in. Usually, in those kinds of instances, it ends up in the outro, but no, they resisted that, too. The riff in the verses would get reworked and used again for 'Highway To Hell'.

'Riff Raff'
The rising power and force of the intro, with Malcolm revving the band up, explodes after a pause into that ferocious spasmodic riff. And what an astoundingly brilliant riff it is. It's a track that Angus picked out to *Loudwire* in 2020 as a personal favourite: 'If I was just thinking of the guitar, since I'm a guitar player, I'd say 'Riff Raff'. The guitar work was a challenge but interesting in the way the song rolled out. That's my guitar answer'. It's interesting that Phil plays a much busier drum track than you might expect

him to, but he is still a real powerhouse. Bon, meanwhile, gives it his all; he really lets rip on this one and he had to if he was going to stamp his authority over the backing track.

The outro is clever, with a slowdown on the riff and a crescendo to finish. It remains one of the quality bench-mark songs in their catalogue; the very essence of what makes AC/DC great is right here. It found its full potential as a key part of the live set but inexplicably got dropped as the band moved into the Brian years. It made its live debut with Brian at the Power Trip gig in October 2023, after the band had played it with Axl Rose in 2016 when he stepped in for Brian.

'Sin City'
The titular city of sin is Las Vegas. As far as the band were concerned, this was 'the big one' from the album. It's a steamroller of a track, with a wild solo from Angus, but there's something lacking in the chorus, which is underwhelming. The contrast between the main parts of the song and the extended breakdown does mark it out as something special. That breakdown (2:37) works really well, with a change of mood and dynamics as the backing track drops to Cliff and Phil. It gives Bon the space and stage and he doesn't disappoint. From there, it's full throttle to the outro, with a clever final subdued bass-heavy payoff.

'What's Next To The Moon'
A very different vibe for this track, with the lead guitar parts in the intro and verses verging on the psychedelic. The chorus is more traditional AC/DC riff-heavy, with great interplay between Bon and the guitar riff. The verse that mentions Superman contains a direct lyrical nod (at 1:16) to the song 'It's A Bird, It's A Plane, It's Superman' from 1954. Bon uses the same phrase, swapping 'suicide' for 'Superman'. The solo (1:36) is unusual because Angus makes rare use of his tremolo, and it sounds great, too! This is the kind of deep cut that is always a joy to discover on AC/DC albums.

'Gone Shootin''
The contrast between the swinging rhythm section groove and the clipped guitars makes this a classic. Cliff's bass is the anchor at the heart of it and the harmony lick Angus plays over Malcolm's riff is lovely. Bon is audibly enjoying every line of it, too, adopting a relaxed approach that fits the groove. Even the solo blends in superbly. There's a lovely part at the end when the riff stops and rings out, then comes back again for a long, joyous fadeout. The song has a fabulous purity to it; it's the real deal, and it deserves to be highly acclaimed as one of the great AC/DC songs.

'Up To My Neck In You'
Very welcome, familiar territory as the Chuck Berry-style shuffle makes another appearance. This blistering rocker is another one that deserves far

more acclaim. The intro is terrific, with a choppy riff and a second ringing riff in harmony. At the 15-second mark, Angus drops down so that his guitar is closer to Malcolm's. It gives the song extra punch as they head into the first verse. There's scarcely any difference between the verses and choruses musically; they just keep that rhythm going.

Bon handles the vocals with effortless power and control. He is utterly convincing as the disgruntled lover. The guitar solo comes in at 1:52 and it's a great complementary solo to the rhythm track. It's a long solo, too, lasting till 3:14. That leaves just enough time for a long outro of verse/chorus repeats to the end. A great song.

'Kicked In The Teeth'
What a way to finish. The attention-grabbing opening vocal salvo tells you they are going to finish the album on a high. The riffs, when the song kicks in, are recycled from 'Let There Be Rock', but we can forgive them for that due to the full-on stun-attack we get here. The chorus, such as it is, is barely different to the verses. This is all about the pummelling assault with Angus's wild lead guitar and Bon's histrionic vocals. The song sounds a lot shorter than it actually is, such is the intensity of it.

Powerage Variations
The UK issue had a different rockier mix on the original vinyl release and opens with 'Gimme A Bullet'. That version included 'Cold Hearted Man' but did *not* feature 'Rock 'N' Roll Damnation'. It was supposedly mixed in haste to get the album out to coincide with a tour. A new version of the album was then released, which dropped 'Cold Hearted Man', added 'Damnation' (in its single edit) and was remixed. There was then, finally, a subsequent remix done for the American market, with the now standard running order as outlined earlier.

UK Only Track
'Cold Hearted Man'
This gave Mark Evans his uncredited appearance on the original LP. With hindsight, you can tell it was recorded earlier; it sounds like the mid-point between *Let There Be Rock* and *Powerage*. It's not a great song and sounds like it's not much past the demo stage. The best thing about it is Malcolm's snapping guitar and the middle-eight, where Angus's riff keeps going round and round over Malcolm's guitar. A good song, but it was rightly eventually replaced on the album.

What Happened Next?
Despite the quality of the songs, *Powerage* didn't get much traction in the setlist. Only 'Sin City' had any real legs in the set. While the band were touring America, they played at Bill Graham's Day *On The Green* festival

on 23 July 1978 at Oakland Coliseum. AC/DC were bottom of the bill, supporting, in ascending order, Van Halen, Pat Travers, Foreigner and Aerosmith. Steve Rosen interviewed Angus and Bon for *Guitar Player*. He asked how the band progressed from their earlier albums. Bon opined that 'the band has a lot of rawness and it (has) progressed, but it hasn't lost its feeling. People criticise us because they say we can't play. I hate bands that go above people's heads. You know, musically, they're trying to put shit on an audience – they're not going with 'em, they're going against 'em. A lot of people take us wrong'. That remained so until the band started to receive acclaim sometime around *Ballbreaker* as a band who were true to their roots.

In Liverpool, the *Echo* (6 May 1978) asked Bon about Angus's schoolboy outfit. 'I think he did it as a joke at first, but then everyone has taken it to their hearts and it's become almost our trademark, which is really quite funny. It's very hard not to fall about laughing at some of the antics he gets up to onstage. He's an incredible guy'. All well and good, and the album and gigs were going down a storm. But necessary changes were ahead.

Highway To Hell (1979)

Personnel:
Bon Scott: lead vocals
Angus Young: lead guitar
Malcolm Young: rhythm guitar, backing vocals
Cliff Williams: bass, backing vocals
Phil Rudd: drums
Robert John 'Mutt' Lange: backing vocals
Produced by Robert John 'Mutt' Lange at Albert Studios, Sydney, Criteria Studios,
Miami and Roundhouse Studios, London, between December 1978 and April
1979
Release date: 27 July 1979
Label: Albert/Atlantic
Highest chart places: Australia: 13, UK: 8, USA: 17
Running time: 41:38
All songs by Angus Young, Malcolm Young and Bon Scott

The big change came with this album, which Browning says 'came down to
Atlantic in America wanting an album that was going to break through. There
were question marks from them, not so much to do with Bon but just in
general. Everyone loved the band live and there were radio stations here and
there that loved them'. Atlantic President Jerry Greenberg suggested a change
of producer. Malcolm put the situation bluntly to *Guitar World* in July 2008:
'Basically, Atlantic, our record label in America, said, 'We're gonna drop you
guys unless you get another producer'. We were selling a couple hundred
thousand copies every time out, but they wanted bigger and better'.

It meant goodbye (for the time being) to George Young and Harry
Vanda. Angus indicated to *Guitar World* in July 2008. that the duo were
philosophical about it: '(They) figured it was a good time for us to go out
in the world and try something new. George always used to say, 'You never
know; somebody out there might have something different to offer you guys'.
I suppose it was a bit like how birds do it; you get kicked out and have to
learn to fly on your own'. Browning's take is that it was harder for the band
than Angus lets on: 'Initially, it was awful. It was one of the lowest points of
the band's career up to that point'. While George was out as producer, he
remained with the band from a distance and would continue to do so. The
family ties remained strong. Angus told *Guitar World* in 2000 that 'every
album we've ever made, whether George was producing or not, we've always
sat down with him and played him the material, either before or during the
recording. He gives us a good idea of where we're at'.

Atlantic's preferred producer was Eddie Kramer, renowned for his work
with Jimi Hendrix and Led Zeppelin. The band had no choice but to give
him a go and so sessions commenced in February 1979 at Criteria Studios,
Miami. After just three days, it was obvious to the band that it wasn't working.

Above: Promo picture from 1974, featuring Neil Smith (bass) on the top left and Noel Taylor (drums) on the bottom left. Dave Evans is in the middle and the Youngs are on the right. (*c/o Noel Taylor*)

Below: The *Black Ice* tour line-up in 2009. The last time around with Malcolm Young. (*Author collection*)

Left: George Young gets his young(er) brothers in on the Marcus Hook Roll Band's *Tales Of Old Grand-Daddy* – a good-time rock 'n' roll album. This is the original cover. (*EMI*)

Right: The debut single 'Can I Sit Next To You Girl?', featuring Dave Evans on vocals. It's a good debut but things were about to mightily improve. (*Albert*)

Left: Their Australian debut album, *High Voltage,* contains a set of songs that show the band's promise, including the fabulous 'Soul Stripper'. (*Albert*)

Right: Full of great songs, *T.N.T.* – their second Australian album – could easily have been issued worldwide just as it is. (*Albert*)

Left: The international version of *High Voltage* is a compilation of the best of the first two albums, intended as a 'starter' for North America and Europe. (*Atlantic*)

Right: The cartoon cover for the 'High Voltage' single, featuring 'It's A Long Way To The Top (If You Wanna Rock 'N' Roll)' on the B-side. (*Atlantic*)

Left: Angus looking mischievous in Melbourne (1975). (*Author collection*)

Below: The line-up with Mark Evans (second left) on bass produced three classic albums. (*Author collection*)

Left: Gerard Huerta's original drawing of the iconic AC/DC logo. (*c/o Gerard Huerta*)

Right: The Australian release of *Dirty Deeds Done Dirt Cheap* has this cartoon cover and also features the magnificent 'Jailbreak'. (*Albert*)

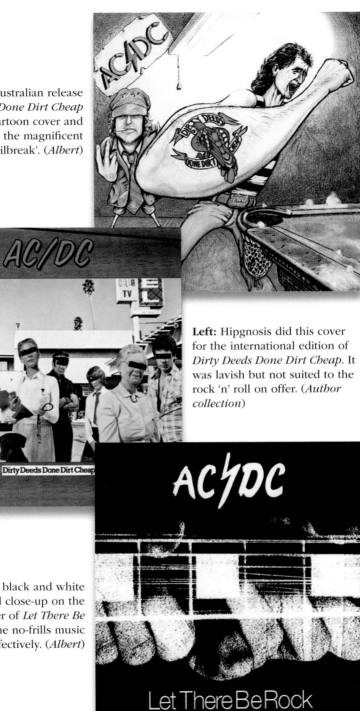

Left: Hipgnosis did this cover for the international edition of *Dirty Deeds Done Dirt Cheap*. It was lavish but not suited to the rock 'n' roll on offer. (*Author collection*)

Right: The black and white fretboard close-up on the Australian cover of *Let There Be Rock* suits the no-frills music effectively. (*Albert*)

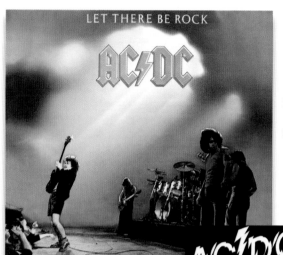

Left: The raw, hard riffing of *Let There Be Rock* sees it remain a fan favourite. (*Atlantic*)

Right: Often picked out as the 'best' with Bon, *Powerage* has a well-rounded selection of songs, still with an edge to them. (*Atlantic*)

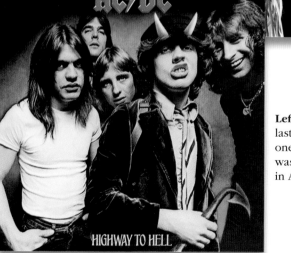

Left: *Highway To Hell* was the last album with Bon and the first one produced by 'Mutt' Lange. It was the big breakthrough album in America. (*Atlantic*)

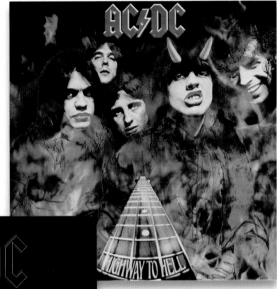

Right: The Australian cover for *Highway To Hell*, with the flames of hell, is arguably superior to the international version. (*Albert*)

Left: *Back In Black* was an astonishing achievement, especially given the circumstances. It's one of the biggest-selling albums of all time. (*Atlantic*)

Right: It was hard to follow *Back In Black*, but *For Those About To Rock* has some great songs, including the classic title track. (*Atlantic*)

Above: A live still of the band at Dundee Caird Hall on 29 May 1978 for the *Powerage* tour. (*Author collection*)

Right: Near the end for Bon. The *Highway To Hell* tour hits Birmingham Odeon. (*Author collection*)

ODEON · THEATRE
BIRMINGHAM

M. C. P. presents
A C / D C
EVENING 7-30 p.m.
FRIDAY
DECEMBER **21**

FRONT STALLS
£3·75
H17

NO TICKET EXCHANGED NOR MONEY REFUNDED
THIS PORTION TO BE RETAINED   [P.T.O.

Left: Bon and Angus in the dressing room at Atlanta Symphony Hall in 1978. Another Coke for Angus? (*Author collection*)

Right: Angus on Bon's shoulders.
Behind them, Malcolm is oblivious!
(*Author collection*)

Below: The boys rocking Oakland
Coliseum on 5 September 1979.
(*Author collection*)

Right: Bon Scott at
Wembley Stadium
on 18 August
1979. The second
Highway To Hell
tour date. (*Author
collection*)

Left: In 1981, *Sounds* tried out a new magazine called *Kerrang!* – Angus was the cover star. (*Author collection*)

Right: Phil Rudd left and was replaced by the youthful Simon Wright (centre). (*Author collection*)

Left: Brian Johnson and engineer Dave Thoener captured during a break in recording the vocals for the *For Those About To Rock* album. (*c/o Dave Thoener*)

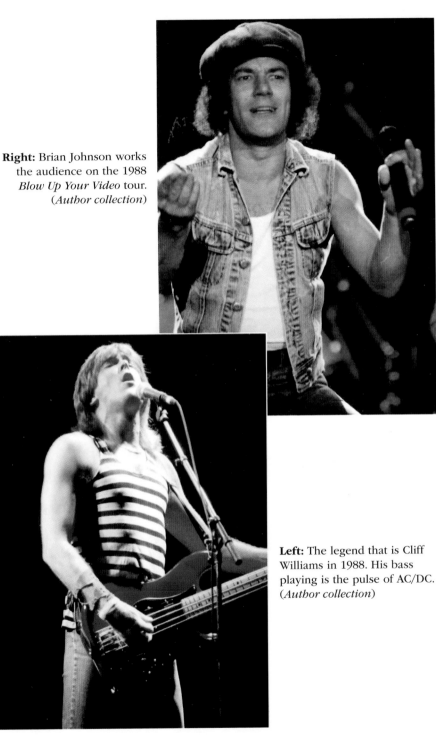

Right: Brian Johnson works the audience on the 1988 *Blow Up Your Video* tour. (*Author collection*)

Left: The legend that is Cliff Williams in 1988. His bass playing is the pulse of AC/DC. (*Author collection*)

Left: Back to basics for the gritty *Flick Of The Switch*, which deserves more acclaim, though the cover took the basic approach too far! (*Atlantic*)

Right: The thin production on *Fly On The Wall* is poor, but there is a shortage of quality tunes anyway. This is the first album with Simon Wright on drums. (*Atlantic*)

Left: The return of Vanda and (George) Young as producers was a boost. A classic in 'Heatseeker' opens *Blow Up Your Video* in style. (*Atlantic*)

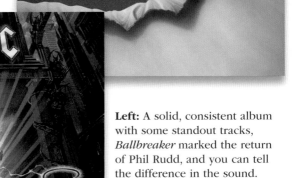

Right: *The Razor's Edge* was seen as a massive return to form, with 'Thunderstruck' standing supreme. Chris Slade made his debut as the drummer. (*Atlantic*)

Left: A solid, consistent album with some standout tracks, *Ballbreaker* marked the return of Phil Rudd, and you can tell the difference in the sound. (*East West*)

Right: The swaggering brilliance of the title track set a high benchmark for *Stiff Upper Lip*. For the most part, this is an excellent album. (*East West*)

Left: Brian and Angus on the *Black Ice* tour. These two will carry the band forward, along with Stevie Young. (*Author collection*)

Right: Chris Slade did a great job on *The Razor's Edge* album and tours. Surprisingly, he came back again for the *Rock Or Bust* tour. (*Author collection*)

Left: Stevie Young covered for Malcolm in 1988 before taking up a permanent position as rhythm guitarist in January 2014. (*Author collection*)

Right: The band's Guv'nor and driver for so many years. It was Malcolm's band. (*Author collection*)

Below: AC/DC always sounded best with Phil Rudd. Here he is at Download festival in 2010. (*Author collection*)

Left: It's overly long and the cover is poor, but *Black Ice* is still a high-quality AC/DC album. The best track, as ever, opens the album. All aboard the 'Rock 'N' Roll Train'! (*Columbia*)

Right: An album without Malcolm seemed unthinkable, but they nailed it on *Rock Or Bust*. Stevie Young emulates his Uncle Malcolm so well. The fierce call-to-arms title track leads the way. (*Columbia*)

Left: Could *Power Up* be the last album? There are no real classics, but it's a strong, enjoyable album. (*Columbia*)

Malcolm summarised what went wrong to *Guitar World* in 2003: 'We showed him (Kramer) the riffs for 'Highway To Hell' and he didn't quite get it. We thought, 'This guy's out of touch with what we are''. Angus added: 'At the same time, I suppose any ideas that Eddie had didn't seem to inspire us. I don't know why, but he kept talking about pianos. Maybe he thought that a piano was an interesting thing for a rock and roll band'. The last straw, it seems, was Kramer's suggestion that they try a cover of the Spencer Davis Group's 'Gimme Some Lovin''. That was the last straw for Malcolm and he rang Browning to sort it out. Browning was in the right place at the right time when the call came:

I was living in an apartment in New York with Mutt Lange and his manager. I got a phone call from Malcolm to say, 'This is not working out with this guy. Get us out of here'. I literally got off the phone, looked at Mutt Lange and said: 'You gotta make the next AC/DC record'. He and his manager didn't really want to know at the time because Mutt was at the stage of his career where he would only agree to produce artists who had a base of 500,000 (Gold) sales. I just kept on talking and convinced him to do it and that's how it happened.

Robert 'Mutt' Lange had little to no rock pedigree, so why did Browning feel he was a good fit? 'The thing that turned me on about him was he played me his wife Stevie Lange's album, which he had recorded, and it was incredible. I didn't tell AC/DC that he was the producer of The Boomtown Rats. If I had, they would have said forget it. I emphasised to them what I had heard about the work he did on his wife's album and said he would be a great producer for them'.

Angus recalled to *Guitar World* in July 2008. that 'Malcolm called (Lange) up and more or less said, 'Well, what can you do for us?' And Mutt had the right answers. He went, 'I don't think you need to be in the studio for a long time'. We had already written most of the tracks for *Highway To Hell*, so Mutt said he'd just give it a bit of spit and polish and we'd be out in five or six weeks'.

Agreement duly reached, Lange accepted the role. As well as his production credentials, he was a consummate musician, songwriter and arranger. But there was no doubt that hooking up with AC/DC was as much of a new experience for him as it was for AC/DC. Browning remembers that 'They went off to England to make that record with Mutt. I went over there for a couple of days to introduce them and make sure everything was okay'.

The first sessions were booked for the Roundhouse Studios in London. The challenge for Lange was how to add more finesse and polish without losing the band's edge. His modus operandi was to demo and rehearse the songs over and over till they were right. The three months or so that they spent recording *Highway To Hell* were the longest they had ever spent on an album to that point. That said, Angus commented to *Guitar World* in July 2008 on the relative speed of recording compared to the next two with Lange: 'We went in and did all the backing tracks in about 13 days or something. In fact, I think that was probably the quickest album we did with him'. There were the occasional heated moments which arose, such as when Lange coaxed more and better out of Bon's voice. But Browning says that he was 'receiving reports that they were getting on like a house on fire'. He was relieved, but not surprised:

> He was such a lovely guy, and there was no way anyone was not going to like him. You could tell he was a really talented musician and I knew he was going to be good for them. That's not to say I thought any the less of the records Vanda and Young had made. It was just that, at that moment, they needed that input from someone new who knew what different radio was about.

Lange's work on making the trademark AC/DC sound more transatlantic without sacrificing too much of their edge is very noticeable. There's the more polished arrangements, which Lange had a huge part in. The songs' rough edges are smoothed out and Bon's vocals are less abrasive. Then there are the refined backing vocals, which are now a big part of the AC/DC sound. Lange, himself, sings on the backups and is easy to hear as the melodic high vocal. In effect, it adds some sweetening to the choruses. He must surely have had a hand in the songwriting, too. All of this comes together in a production and mix that is more palatable for a mass audience. Consequently, this is the album that saw AC/DC hit the premier league of the big rock bands.

The title track inspired the album cover, which had no Satanic agenda. The influence for the lyrics was instead the rigours of life on the road. Angus elaborated to *Guitar World* in 1993 that 'when you're sleeping with the singer's socks two inches from your nose, that's pretty close to hell'. What *is* surprising is that Atlantic went with the title and an admittedly sanitised but still provocative cover when they were so invested in breaking the band. The less controversy, the better you would have thought, so it's to their credit that they gave the band their head on this.

The front cover exists in two versions, with Australia getting the best one. The colourised band are surrounded by the flames of hell and a fretboard in the foreground doubles as the titular highway. The colours are vibrant and the Huerta logo is a vivid red with yellow line edging and accents. The International cover is more formal. The band shot (by Jim Houghton) is retained with muted colouring and that's it, apart from one detail. Angus's horns and tail are still in place but were obviously felt to be an acceptable, amusing touch, highlighted by Bon's laughing face. Also present and hard to ignore is Angus's awesome stiff upper lip! Interestingly, the cover picture was not 'new'; they made use of an unused photo from the *Powerage* photo sessions. The back cover picture of the band, also by Houghton, *was* new.

In the final analysis, this album is obviously a bridge between their earlier albums and *Back In Black*. Yet, I don't think it is their best album with Bon; that, I feel, would be *Powerage*. Although *Highway* is solidly great on side one, it's more of a mixed bag on side two. But the barnstorming title track connected with a new audience, who lapped up the album.

When the sessions were over, Browning recalled: 'I was in New York and the band brought in a cassette of the album and played it to me. I heard 'Highway To Hell' and I was like, 'Woah, this is the track; this is the one that's gonna do it for them'. It broke them worldwide to the level that Atlantic expected. The question of how they would follow it turned out to have a tragic beginning with an astonishing conclusion.

'Highway To Hell'

For such a huge track in their catalogue, it is built on surprisingly little foundations. It opens with Malcolm's rhythm guitar, joined by Phil's drums, and then in comes Bon for the first verse. Verse two arrives and it's *still* that configuration. The minimal backing track makes the riff sound bigger and Bon's delivery more of a focal point. Lange and the band hold back on the full-throttle attack until the chorus. Only then do Angus, Cliff and the backing vocals come in for that huge swelling roar. Everything is thrown at the chorus. But what's interesting is that they don't build on that chorus at this point. For the third verse ('No stop signs') and then the fourth ('Hey Satan'), it's back again to basics, followed by the big chorus.

Angus's solo comes in at 2:12 and has an almost country feel to it. It's not the big beast of a solo you might expect here and it's surprisingly short for what became such a big song. He is there, though, adding fills and licks all the way through the outro, which is effectively one long chorus. There's a lovely pause for Angus's sharp fill at 2:42, but otherwise, there's no interruption.

This is one of their biggest and very best songs and drove the album and ticket sales up. The single charted everywhere, even reaching number four in the UK. It was backed with either 'If You Want Blood' or 'Night Prowler', depending on where it was released.

'Girls Got Rhythm'

This is a revealing song for the differences that Lange made to AC/DC. It's a rocker that would have sat easily on the tracklists for any of the three or four albums before it, but Lange's touches give it a catchy, almost pop feel that dials down the rawness. Lange's work on the harmony lead and backing vocals smooths the choruses out, too. It's acclaimed by many as one of the best tracks on the album, but, in truth, it misses the sharp edges it would have had pre-Lange. The immediate evidence is the intro, which is almost polite when it needs to roar. Angus's solo injects some excitement, but the song still sounds reined in. Despite the catchiness of the song, it failed to chart anywhere as a single.

'Walk All Over You'

This is more like it, the most live-sounding track on the album, which nods back to the Vanda/Young productions. A long, slow intro says this is going to get big and loud. Phil is superb here; his drums are the prominent feature over the backing guitar riffs. That first big guitar chord after 13 seconds is great, and then you get the eventual release as everything boils over as the tipping point is reached at 0:50. And, oh my, they kill it from here on with a pulsating racket and Bon hammering out the lyrics.

The chorus backing vocal is pure Lange; you can hear the same thing he works with Def Leppard here. You can also hear him clearly at the top end of the vocals. He's a really good singer and the band have never been as tuneful on backing vocals since they parted company with him! Angus's solo is straight out of his top drawer, easily one of the best on the album. He absolutely rips it out. They finish it with one of those big crescendos they do so well. A marvellous track!

'Touch Too Much'

Although the band never performed it live at the time, its commercial potential was noted and it was released as a single. You can see them mime to it on *TOTP* shortly before Bon passed away.

It features (among others) the great opening couplet from Bon: 'It was one of those nights when you turn off the lights and everything comes into view'.

The song sees the band veering more towards a radio-friendly rock/pop sound, hence the single release. The poppy groove on the verses was a new thing for the band, while the catchy chorus raised that bar even higher. In spite of this, there's still enough dirt in the riffs to keep the edges rough. Angus's solo (2:17) goes straight for the jugular as a direct contrast to all this tunefulness. It's followed by the bridge (2:38), which might be the best part of the song. It's got a great call-and-response vocal between Angus and the others, with the rhythm trio keeping the motors running. The song feels like it needed a bit of editing, certainly as a single, but otherwise, this is a good song that indicates the kind of territory AC/DC would increasingly occupy in the Brian years.

It was released as a single/EP, with 'Live Wire' and 'Shot Down In Flames' on the B-side, recorded at Hammersmith Odeon on 2 November 1979. Both would later appear on *Backtracks*.

'Beating Around The Bush'

Peter Green's riff to part one of Fleetwood Mac's 'Oh Well' is surely the inspiration here. Malcolm comes in first on one side of the stereo spectrum and is then doubled by Angus on the other. The tempo is furious but precision-tight, with Bon singing between the guitar riffs in the verses. The chorus is more of an interruption; there's not much to it; this song is very much about the verses. After the first verse and chorus, Malcolm keeps the riff going while Angus plays licks around him. The first solo (1:52) section is a real nod back to the *Let There Be Rock* album, with the band hitting the full-on aggression that permeates that album. But there's room for some wicked asides here in the maelstrom; Bon's 'the rest is up to – you!' is direct and playful. Angus's second solo (3:05) is the spice added to the outro, which features a fabulous crescendo.

The Netherlands got this great track as a single.

'Shot Down In Flames'

A solid song that has been a live set staple. The opening guitar that 'winds up' the song is too low in the mix, making for an anti-climactic start. A brief pause, then in comes the big riff (with added volume) and a cry of 'woah' from someone, followed by a further ecstatic 'Woah' from Bon, which says we are now in business! There's a real groove in the rhythm, which contrasts well against Malcolm's choppy rhythm. Angus comes in and doubles the rhythm, breaking off from it for a little lick that keeps things interesting. That lick always introduces the chorus and features strongly on it, too. The chorus is powerful, albeit it lacks that extra bite to make it hit home with more impact. Bon gives one of his strongest performances on the album on this song. Angus matches him, too, with a scorching solo. It's not an AC/DC classic; the chorus isn't quite great enough, but it's a really good song.

'Get it Hot'

The riff is naggingly familiar. It's easily one of the weaker songs on the album, with little to offer of substance. Strangely, the chorus doesn't 'big it up', though Bon does his best to make it work. Lange resisted a gang backing vocal for it when there really ought to have been one. The song sounds undercooked and a bit messy, as though it hasn't quite come together.

'If You Want Blood (You've Got It)'

The title came easily enough from the live album and the song itself is one of those that harks back to the pre-*Highway* era. The riff is great and sets the tone for some swinging, lively verses. The chorus lacks a touch of class and they resort to a gang-style vocal that doesn't quite do it. The verses are way more interesting, and that's quite unusual for AC/DC. Even the solo isn't really one of Angus's best. File it under 'good but could have done better'. An early version of the song, with some different lyrics, appears on *Bonfire*.

The song was used in the last scene and closing credits of FX's show *The Bear*. Executive Producer Josh Senior told *Billboard* in July 2023: 'Everybody I've ever talked to about licensing music always told me AC/DC was hard to get, hard to pay for, hard to contact, hard to deal with. And we knew we

69

wanted that song. They ended up being amazing and awesome. But the hype was intimidating'.

'Love Hungry Man'

Angus has said it's one of his least favourite AC/DC songs, which must come down to the poppy feel of it and the funky groove from Cliff and Phil. He has a good point, but the fact is that it is a hell of a groove, with a very rare chance for Cliff to show off some different chops. It's the busiest bass playing he has ever done for the band. It's not obvious from the crashing intro where it's going, so it comes as a surprise when the rhythm comes in. The backing vocals are terrific, too, courtesy of Lange, who is very audible on the harmonies. So, an atypical song for them, which, whisper it quietly, you could imagine as a disco-style mix. I like the song very much and it could have been an edited single. How they got the track to 4:17 in length for the album is quite a feat!

'Night Prowler'

It could have been a much better last song on the album; it's one that never quite seems to grab me. It sees the band stretching out on a long, slow blues. Phil swings it nicely and adds a deliberate, almost lazy feel and texture. Angus also underplays it with a woozy opening solo. Bon sounds like he has been out all night, the worse for wear, in the verses. Lange sensitively uses the backing vocals to add lighter tones to the chorus and this works well. Bon signs off for some reason with 'Shazbot, Nanu Nanu' – two of Robin Williams's catchphrases from the *Mork And Mindy* TV show.

The song has become somewhat sidelined due to its unfortunate connection to the serial killer Richard Ramirez, who was known as the 'Night Stalker'. Ramirez was arrested on 31 August 1985 and his interest in AC/DC, and especially this song, was noted. Police claimed that Ramírez was wearing an AC/DC shirt and even left an AC/DC hat at one of his crime scenes. For a time, it caused the band problems; they maintained to *Behind The Music* that 'Night Prowler' had been misinterpreted by Ramírez, as the band insisted that it is about a boy sneaking into his girlfriend's bedroom at night.

Related Tracks
'Back Street Confidential'

This song was abandoned, but the riffs were kept for 'Beating Around The Bush'. It's a raw take on the track, with the lead guitar even more in your face. The roots of the main riff in Fleetwood Mac's 'Oh Well' are even easier to discern here than on 'Beating Around The Bush'. The intro doesn't really catch fire and it's only when the riff comes in at 0:47 that things pick up. It's a great riff, of course, and they could, and should, have kicked the song straight off from it. From here, it sounds musically similar to the released version, although the lyrics are entirely different. The chorus doesn't quite make it simply because the title doesn't scan well. It's a curio worth hearing and is available on *Bonfire*.

'Get It Hot'

Same title as on the album, but this song has different lyrics and music. It's a shame this was discarded because it has bite and conviction, with a Stones 'Brown Sugar' feel to it in the intro and verses. The chorus is good, but a stronger title and a bit more lift to it would have worked wonders. Otherwise, the band are on fire and there's a great solo from Angus. I would rate this more highly, as it is, than at least two or three that made the final album cut. It's also on *Bonfire*.

What Happened Next?

Happy news following the recording sessions came with Malcolm marrying his girlfriend O'Linda Susan Irish (yes, her real name) in Westminster, London (registered between April and June 1979). Less happy was the departure of Michael Browning. The band dispensed with his services and signed on with the Leber-Krebs agency, with Peter Mensch as their new manager. Browning is prosaic about it now: 'My relationship fell apart, the energy was not good and I had to go. They got a big American management company, which they probably really needed at that time'.

Browning had been there for all of the band's big moves to that date: 'Yeah, I would agree. It was a really interesting journey breaking the band big in Australia and they became huge there. So, that was a great ride and then Atlantic Records and the UK thing, and Europe was another one of them, and then America'. Browning's excellent book *Dog Eat Dog* explores his time with the band in more detail.

On the back of the album, the band toured heavily across North America and Europe and it seemed clear that the potential was there for them to consolidate and move on to bigger shows and a bigger audience for their music. There was realistically only one fly in the ointment at this point and that was their talismanic singer and his alcohol consumption. I saw them at Birmingham Odeon on a two-night stand in December 1979. The band were great, although I was perplexed as to why they turned the lights down between every song – something they would continue to do in future. There was barely a hint of a stage show other than Angus's striptease and the walkabout. Although, they did bring on two strippers on either side of Phil's kit for 'The Jack'! However, it was clear from my position leaning on the stage that Bon was not in full control. His performance was still there, but his grasp of the lyrics was off at times and he looked and sounded like he was just about on top of the alcohol. It was clearly obvious that he had been drinking heavily. Just two months later, he was gone.

Back In Black (1980)

Personnel:
Brian Johnson: lead vocals
Angus Young: lead guitar
Malcolm Young: rhythm guitar, backing vocals
Cliff Williams: bass, backing vocals
Phil Rudd: drums
Robert John 'Mutt' Lange: backing vocals
Mike Milsom: bell-ringer on 'Hells Bells'
Produced by Robert John 'Mutt' Lange at Compass Point Studios, Nassau,
between April and May 1980
Release date: 25 July 1980
Label: Albert/Atlantic
Highest chart places: Australia: 1, UK: 1, USA: 7
Running time: 42:11
All songs by Angus Young, Malcolm Young and Brian Johnson

The run-up to recording the album got off to a good start, with Angus
marrying his girlfriend Ellen Van Lochem in Westminster, London. The
register has her name as Ella and the marriage took place in early 1980.
By February 1980, Angus and Malcolm had the bare bones of at least two
songs – 'Have A Drink On Me' and 'Let Me Put My Love Into You'. They
worked these up at E-Zee Hire Studios at 6 Hazlitt Mews in Kensington,
London. Bon turned up and played drums in what turned out to be his last
session with the Youngs. Angus was asked by *Total Guitar* in 2020 if Bon
had contributed to the writing of the album: 'Bon wrote a little of the stuff a
week before he died. We started writing the music with Bon on drums. He
was a drummer originally. He'd bang away while me and Malcolm worked
out the riffs'.

Bon got in one final recording, on 13 February, with Trust, who recorded a
version of 'Ride On' at London's Scorpio Studios. Bon shared the lead vocals
with Trust's Bernie Bonvoisin and the song can be heard on YouTube.

Bon's death, on 19 February 1980 in East Dulwich, London, from alcohol
poisoning, was a shock but not a surprise. Michael Browning's view is that
'He drank a lot and there's been speculation of other things around his death,
but I don't think so. I think he was just into recreational party stuff. He lived
for the moment, and that's how he lived his life. He would always make the
comment that he wanted to be a good-looking corpse'. New manager Peter
Mensch grimly told the *Sunday Times* in October 2012 that his first job as
manager was identifying Bon's body in the morgue.

The funeral was held in Fremantle, Australia on 1 March. Angus and
Malcolm spent some time before and after it with Bon's parents. Angus told
Classic Rock in 2005: 'I remember Bon's dad saying to Malcolm and me: 'You
must continue with AC/DC. You're young guys, you're on the brink of major

success and you can't afford to give up now'. But, I'll be honest with you, we weren't really listening; we were so wrapped up in our own grief'.

On the flight back to the UK after Bon's funeral, Mensch approached Malcolm with a list of possible new singers. It was way too early for Malcolm to think about it, telling *Classic Rock* in 2005: 'I just couldn't be bothered. I remember waving them away and just thinking it's not fucking right, you know?'

The staggering thing about the situation is how the band managed to recruit a new singer and get an album written, recorded and released in such a short time following Bon's death. Not any old album either, but *Back In Black* – one of the biggest-selling albums of all time.

Choosing the right vocalist wasn't easy. Auditions were held in March 1980 at E-Zee Hire. One maybe possible candidate was Iggy Pop. He told the *New York Times* in 2023 that:

> They had a manager many years ago when I hadn't reformed The Stooges and I hadn't moved to England. And this guy said, 'Are you interested in joining AC/DC?' They were looking for a singer. I listened to their record. I thought, I can't fit that bill. I wasn't, like, 'Ugh, I don't like them'. It was quite well made. They do careful work, but I'm not what they needed.

Iggy didn't specify that it was during the time after Bon's death; it could have been during the difficult period when Atlantic USA rejected *Dirty Deeds*. In fact, that would make more sense, except, it seems, to Michael Browning, who says, 'I had never heard that Iggy Pop thing and it was total news to me'. Definitely a possible was Slade's gravel-voiced leader Noddy Holder. He confirmed the story to *Planet Rock* in 2020:

> They approached my management to ask whether I'd like to join AC/DC. I think they probably heard that Slade was sort of on the verge of breaking up and I was approached to join them. I said I'd turn it down, you know; I still got it in my head that Slade was still a force to be reckoned with and that we'd still be carrying on. But I would have turned it down anyway because Slade was my baby.

Other names considered included Terry Wilson-Slesser, who the Youngs knew from AC/DC gigs as support to Slesser's band Back Street Crawler. Then, from Australia, there was Jimmy Barnes, John Swan and, best of all, Stevie Wright (ex. Easybeats) – someone well-known to the Youngs. Also known was Wright's issues with drugs, and this made him uncomfortably similar, in that respect, to Bon Scott. There was one Aussie who got close to the job. Browning says: 'There was a guy called Allan Fryer, who I ended up managing in a band called Heaven. He was touted as being a potential replacement. The furthest he got was an audition with Vanda and Young in

Sydney. They liked him, but the band had their hearts set on Brian Johnson'. Fryer, at that time, was lead vocalist with Aussie band Fat Lip.

Back with UK candidates, the former Heavy Metal Kids singer Gary Holton would have been a great fit, but his issues with alcohol and substance abuse ruled him out. Another who came close was Steve 'Burtie' Burton, a roadie from Birmingham who was recommended by AC/DC's crew. Burton got to audition but lost out to Brian Johnson. Burton told *Rock Candy* in 2021: 'I must have made an impression on the band because soon afterwards, I got a call asking if I'd be interested in working with Angus and Malcolm Young's nephew Stevie. He was putting a new band together in Birmingham, and Malcolm had told him he should get hold of me'. That band was Starfighters, who supported AC/DC on the UK leg of the *Back In Black* tour.

Brian Johnson, the lead vocalist with glam-rock band Geordie, was back home in Newcastle living with his parents in 1980. Now aged 32, he felt his chance of the big-time was long gone. By day, he made a living from repairing vinyl roofs of classic cars while keeping his hand in recording vocals for TV commercials. The call to audition for AC/DC was a complete and welcome shock. He recalled, in his first 'autobiography' *Rockers And Rollers*, what happened when he arrived.

> In the rehearsal room sat the boys of AC/DC, looking quite bored. They'd been auditioning singers for a month. When I walked in, I introduced myself and Malcolm said, 'Ah, you're the Newcastle lad', and promptly gave me a bottle of Newcastle Brown Ale. He said, 'Well, what do you wanna sing?' I told him 'Nutbush City Limits' by Tina Turner.

That was a surprise to the band, and with everyone now warmed up, they blasted through 'Whole Lotta Rosie' and 'Highway To Hell'. Job done and Brian was called back for a second audition. He was asked to come up with some lyrics for 'Given The Dog A Bone' for this audition. This fact is not often mentioned, but it does show that Brian could write lyrics under pressure. A frontman who could contribute to the writing was a vital part of the role. Many accounts give the impression that the lyric writing was dropped on Brian when they arrived at Compass Point Studios for the *Back In Black* recording sessions, but both Malcolm and Angus would have had ideas in advance.

Brian got the job in March 1980 and was officially announced, ironically, as the new vocalist on 1 April. A week or so later, he was on his way to Compass Point in the Bahamas to work on the album! The rest of the band were waiting and had started work on the backing tracks.

While it was obviously an immensely difficult time for the band, the man with the hardest job was Brian. He was thrown into recording with scarcely any notice. While he had the chops and confidence to handle the vocals, he must have been concerned with the timescale in which to come up with the lyrics. His credits for lyrics with Geordie say that he wrote (or co-wrote) nine songs over four albums. So he could do it (kind of) and there is no doubt that Angus, Malcolm and Mutt Lange had input as well. Lange's contributions to the arranging and songwriting were huge.

On whom might or might not have written material other than Brian, Browning says: 'I would think *Back In Black* might have been Malcolm's title. Malcolm used to come up with song titles and riffs and then Bon would get involved, so I think he would have done that too with Brian'.

The big question is whether Bon's much-reported notebook of ideas was 'made available' too. The late Malcolm Dome said in *Classic Rock* in 2005 that he personally saw at least one line from the album in Bon's notebook:

> Bon proudly showed me some scribbles he'd put down in preparation for an album he felt would define AC/DC and open up new possibilities. It's hard to be absolutely accurate from a distance of a quarter of a century and through the haze of alcohol which enveloped the night, but one line sticks in my mind as being on one of those sheets: 'She told me to come, but I was already there'.

Angus effectively substantiated the existence of those notes in his July 2008 interview with *Guitar World*: '(Bon) was actually supposed to come in that same week he died. He had this pile of lyrics he'd been kicking about and he said, 'Well, maybe I could come in and try out some ideas'.' If the 'pile of lyrics' were found in Bon's flat, Angus insisted in a fan Q&A on *Reddit* in 2014 that 'Anything he left went back to his family. Any notes he had ever left or messages. Anything that was there that was his all went to his family'. The question is whether they were looked at first and used. In the same interview, Angus revealed a little about the origins of some of the songs:

> Some stuff, like 'Hells Bells', was obviously written with Bon in mind, but then a lot of it was written when Bon was still around. I remember during the *Highway To Hell* tour, Malcolm came in one day and played me a couple of ideas he had knocked down on cassette, and one of them was the main riff for 'Back In Black'. And he said, 'Look, it's been bugging me, this track. What do you think?' He was going to wipe it out and reuse the tape because cassettes were sort of a hard item for us to come by sometimes! I said, 'Don't trash it. If you don't want it, I'll have it'.

What is undeniable is that AC/DC's lyrics are simpler and more obvious in terms of the rhymes than they were with Bon. Yet, other than 'You Shook Me All Night Long', there's nothing that is as 'clever' on *Back In Black* as the best of Bon's lyrics. There's not much on the later albums either ('Spellbound' being another possible exception). This is not to knock the lyrics per se; they do what they do and they do it effectively, but you don't get that way with words that Bon had. Bon's lyrics came from his observations and experiences of life and he covered a lot of emotional territory in them too. Bon comes over as a thoughtful writer most of the time and he knew how to put it across well. The era with Brian loses that; the lyrics are less interesting and often just seem written to fit a title with little thought other than that.

The sequencing of the album is ingenious. The four big bangers are 'Hells Bells' and 'Shoot To Thrill', which open side one, and 'Back In Black' and 'You Shook Me All Night Long', which open side two. That sets up each side with the very best on offer, a clever decision that goes some way to making the album as big as it is. They could, for example, have moved 'You Shook Me' onto side one and 'boosted' it, which would have been understandable. The title track is so well-placed to open side two and it works as a pun, too: you've turned the record over and are back (in black).

The title is perfect and the cover dovetails with it as a tribute to Bon. But at the time, it was a brave decision for an album that was so key for them. The album was very noticeable in the shops, all in black with the raised lettering. It had a classy look and 'importance' to it. But there were clues that it had been made fast in the packaging. The inner bag features live shots of the four musicians (presumably from the 1979 tours), but there had been no time to get a picture of Brian live. Instead, he is standing against a wall at E-Zee Studios, tipping his cap. In a further nod to their most totemic member, Angus is at the centre of the spread and, by far, has the largest photo.

All of the band step up with career-best performances. Angus always stands out because of his press allure, but the solos he plays on this album are amongst the best he has ever put together. He explained to *Guitar World* in July 2008 that.

...some were totally off the top, and there were some that I took a bit longer with. With Mutt, he'd just listen and tell you when he thought something was great. Sometimes, I'd be there for a whole day doing one guitar solo, and then he'd go, 'Remember what you were playing at the beginning?' And I'd have to go all the way back to the start.

The album must be the most incredible turnaround in a band's fortunes ever, and it has resulted in it being the second-biggest-selling album of all time. It's also the best one with Brian, of that there is no doubt. And that must have been, and still is, something to give them cause to ponder. They have never come close to equalling it.

But is it better than anything with Bon? That's a tougher call because the band are such a different beast from Bon to Brian. Yes, the elements of AC/DC are there, but the vocal style and performance of the pair make it hard to compare. But when all is said and done, *Back In Back* really is their best album. Play it through again, start to finish, and there is a quality which they have never topped, though there are several excellent other albums in the years after it.

Angus, who contributes arguably his consistently best work on the album, was asked by *Guitar World* in July 2008 why he thought the album had connected with so many people:

At the time, I suppose there was a lot of curiosity. The fans were buying it because they were eager to see how it would be different from what they knew. And then the songs themselves were special. When we were in the studio, we were thinking it could be our last record, so that was a big push. When you lose somebody like Bon, who's a very upfront guy, he was the identity of the band for a lot of people. We didn't know if we could get past that. We knew we had good songs, but even so, you can have great songs, but at the end of the day, people can still go, 'Yeah, whatever'.

The band unquestionably got it right with Brian. He ticked all the boxes for what they needed – vocal prowess, easy-going, big personality, able to write – he fitted in. What he didn't have was Bon's way with a phrase and he didn't have as nuanced a delivery as Bon. But with the songs they were writing, these elements didn't matter so much.

Michael Browning's view is that '*Back In Black* will go down in history as probably the best rock record ever made. It's quite phenomenal. It caught everyone by surprise'.

'Hells Bells'
Brian has referred to 'writer's block' during the sessions. As a tropical storm hit Compass Point, Mutt Lange, says Brian, commented on the thunder. 'Rolling thunder', said Brian, was what they called it in Britain. Inspiration hit and he was off, telling Dan Rather of *The Big Interview* in 2019 that he 'literally was giving a weather report', and it works brilliantly.

Opening with the tolling bell was a brave but powerful tribute to Bon. The plan was to have a two-ton bronze bell specially cast, which could be used for the recording and then taken on tour. The Taylor Foundry in Loughborough, Leicestershire, were approached in April 1980 to manufacture it. Bell master Mike Milsom talked them into a more practical one-ton bell tuned to E. This was pitch-corrected to C for the recording.

With time of the essence, it looked as though Taylor might miss the deadline, so they looked at recording the bell in the Loughborough WW1 Carillon Memorial Tower. While they could have recorded at night to avoid traffic noise, there was no way to avoid the noise from the roosting pigeons in the carillon. Fortunately, Taylor made the deadline, and instead, they recorded the bell they had made in the Foundry. It was Milsom himself who got to ring the bell and make his mark on the album. Live, it would be Brian Johnson who struck the bell, but over the years, this was altered so a recording was played instead.

The opening tolling bell represents a solemn goodbye, but as soon as the band, and especially Brian, come in, this is as much about the present and the future but with a respectful, muted tone. I vividly remember the first time I heard the song. What struck me quickly was that this was a different AC/DC, not just the song but the band itself. They sounded like they had grown as a band. The elements are there from before, but I couldn't imagine how this song would have been possible in the Bon era. The sound is far more polished and 'corporate', but there is also an impressive growth from *Highway To Hell*. This is a song that sounds and feels much bigger than anything they have done before, including 'Highway To Hell' itself. The descending riff by Angus works seamlessly with the tolling bell, and when the rhythm section come in, it's an awesome force of nature. The chorus, with the return of that descending riff, is fabulous. Overall, it's a stunning song and the studio version reigns supreme. It loses some of its stately potency in live versions because the band tend to up the tempo, blurring some of the passages.

It was released as the second single from the album. Trivia note: The apostrophe is missing from hells, but it does look better as a rhyming couplet without it!

'Shoot To Thrill'
It quickly became one of the big audience favourites from the album and has remained a definite inclusion on every setlist since. The twin rhythm playing of the Youngs, the combination of the drawn-out riff from Angus and the choppier one from Malcolm, makes for a great start. What catches your ear quickly is the quirky arrangement, with that rhythm as the basis. The chorus is supremely catchy, with a melodic riff all of its own. Central to the song's reputation is the much beloved mid-song breakdown, which has become a high point of every live gig. Brian's 'play to kill' cues up the breakdown at 3:23. Phil is supreme here, keeping that dynamite groove going while Angus takes off for guitar nirvana. It's one of the very best things AC/DC have ever put together in what is also one of their very best songs.

'What Do You Do For Money Honey'
Another great riff opens this one with that patent Malcolm Young precision guitar. After the dramatic opening, it settles down into the verse groove, which always feels like it's going to head into a great chorus. You can just sense something big is coming. The transition from the verses into the chorus is so smooth and they dial things right up for the chorus, which has those great wall-of-sound backing vocals. Angus' solo is sublime, especially as he drops away from the high notes down the fretboard.

'Given The Dog A Bone'
There's a buzzing confidence about the glorious intro riff that speaks volumes. Four tracks in and the quality hasn't dropped at all. There's the briefest cue from Phil as Malcolm's riff comes in, followed by Angus doubling

the riff. This is so damn good that you could pretty much sing anything over it, but Brian (with possible contributions from the Youngs) opts for sexual congress. The unsubtle metaphoric title is abandoned completely in the verses, which make it crystal clear what is taking place with the innuendo. Despite the problematic title - the lyrics, the backing track and Angus's solo are terrific, and you can't fault Brian's enthusiastic performance.

'Let Me Put My Love Into You'

This is an underrated track! The slow, brooding pace has a sad but dramatic tone to it, which is a surprise given the title. This is a welcome example of AC/DC bypassing and surprising your expectations. Full marks, too, to Brian, who shines in one of his best performances ever for AC/DC.

The intro is reminiscent of 'Hells Bells' and gives side one of the album a feel of everything coming full circle. The verses have a stately but musical feel and there's a great little lick from Angus between Brian's phrases that connects each verse to the chorus. There's a restraint still present in the chorus; they don't go over the top as might be expected from the title. Equally, Angus's solo (2:37) is also an exercise in tasteful restraint, a lyrical and melodic solo that fits the song perfectly. He doesn't really stop the solo as such; a brief pause and he's back stretching out over the outro, which is the perfect ensemble ending to a great song.

'Back In Black'

'Malcolm had that riff for about three weeks', Angus told *Classic Rock* in 2000:

He came in one night and said, 'You got your cassette here? Can I put this down? It's been driving me mad. I won't be getting any sleep until I put it on cassette'. He sat down and played it all. The funniest thing is, he said to me, 'What do you think? I don't know if it's crap or not'.

What Malcolm came up with was one of the catchiest big beast riffs ever written, while the song itself is utterly brilliant – a genuine rock classic. The clipped guitar rhythm and Phil's hi-hat in the intro set up that titanic riff and the descending lick that tails it back to the top. Brian gets close to rapping the verses, which, combined with that riff, gives the song a real 'down on the streets' vibe. There's a confident arrogance that oozes out of it, so it's curious that it's been said to be a tribute to Bon. Nothing about the lyrics has any suggestion of that. Browning concurs, 'When I heard the track 'Back In Black', it said to me that it was the band's statement: 'we're out of debt'.'

The song uses the same trick as on 'Highway To Hell' of keeping the backing track minimal in the verses and pushing everything into the chorus for maximum effect. Lyrically, it's one of the most minimal choruses they have ever done, but it's an absolute monster. Angus pulls off two great solos; the first (1:48) weaves around the rhythm expertly. A series of descending riffs at

2:50 cue up the outro, which features the second solo (3:30), where Angus goes walkabout on his fretboard for a jubilant, melodic solo.

It was the fourth single from the album and might have done better with stronger live B-side selections instead of 'What Do You Do For Money Honey'.

'You Shook Me All Night Long'

It's one of their greatest songs, an absolute classic, and arguably their biggest hit with a wider audience. Brian's lyrical inspiration, he has often said, came from watching TV while they were recording the album. Two American ladies caught his attention and he got writing.

Now, it's definitely one of the high points of his lyric writing, but it's also the song that has attracted the most suspicion in terms of who wrote it. Brian explained the song's origins to *Absolute Radio* in 2021: 'Malcolm and Angus said, 'Listen, we've got this song. It's called 'Shook Me All Night Long'. That's what we want the song to be called'.' And if you listen to the chords, it (the chorus) just fell into place, so I can't claim any credit on that thing'. Brian loved the riff as soon as he heard it: 'I still think it's one of the greatest rock 'n' roll riffs I've ever heard in my life'.

The song opens with a twangy, melodic riff, which has a second guitar part harmonising with it. Phil's drums shatter that and cue in the song's main riff, a staccato catchy thing of wonder! Phil is amazing at this point, just him, Malcolm and then Brian. Verse two sees Angus come in to harmonise on the riff and then, finally, Cliff enters in the chorus. That chorus has it all – a pop/rock crossover and a catchy tune that you can't forget. The backing vocals here are interesting because they sound more raucous and less refined than you might expect. All this and a killer solo from Angus to seal the deal. This might well be the best of the very best AC/DC songs.

It was released as the first single and should have been a massive worldwide hit, but it barely even got into the UK or USA Top 40 singles.

'Have A Drink On Me'

Lyrically, this is a strange one. It's hard not to think of Bon in terms of the title and the lyrics, and that feels a little awkward, given the manner of his death. Yet, the band, and probably Bon, would argue this is what he would have laughed at and wanted from the band.

A stinging, bluesy intro riff is swept away by the band coming in on the riff. The verses work well with the rhythm guitar, cushioning Brian's vocals. They don't waste time in getting to the chorus but it's less effective as it doesn't do much more than the verses. The star of this song is Brian, who delivers the lyrics with real gusto. It's a big performance from him, showcasing his range and delivery. The outro, with everyone on full throttle, is the best part of the song and a real wall of noise. This is still, though, one of the less amazing songs on the album.

'Shake A Leg'

It's magic right from the intro, with Phil just behind the beat against Cliff and Malcolm's rhythm. In comes Brian and the open spaces in the rhythm allow his voice to stand out. The first verse is like a coiled spring waiting for the music to let go, which it finally does at 0:33 with Brian's cry of 'Don't kick don't fight don't sleep at night, and shake a leg'. Ten seconds later, after some stabbing riffs and an increasingly excited Brian, we are off. Phil's turnaround on the kit cues the wild and crazy riff that the song is well-known for, the band playing with a pace and intensity. The solo comes in at 2:26 over a detour from the main riff, winding up with some blisteringly fast notes.

Trivia note: The lyrics (1:59) 'stop your grinnin' and drop your linen' are spoken by Bill Paxton (as Private Hudson) in *Aliens* during the scene where he locates the colonists' transmitters.

'Rock And Roll Ain't Noise Pollution'

This was the last track recorded for the album, and it feels like a final farewell to Bon. Under pressure to finish the album, Malcolm apparently came up with the bones of the song in just 15 minutes. For me, it's the closest they get to a filler track. It starts off great; Brian nails the intro completely, getting across a genuine warmth as he lights up and extemporises while Angus and Phil accompany him. The crash-in of the full band and those twin rhythm guitars hit hard, but I find the verses a little pedestrian in spite of the music, and the chorus just doesn't give me a lift.

Fundamentally, it's the title that lets it down. You hear it a lot, as you expect to, in any AC/DC song, but it hasn't got the weight or gravitas. It's not a bad song, but I don't think it was good enough. Atlantic liked it enough, though, to make it the third single from the album.

Conclusion

The question of whether Brian would be accepted by the fans as the new vocalist came down, in the first instance, to how good the album was. No problems there! On stage, Brian was, and is, a different character to Bon. Whereas Bon seemed like a wayward but irrepressible older brother figure, Brian has always seemed a more avuncular figure – good-natured, sometimes embarrassing, but much loved. He was born to fill the role that he was given. In fact, I would question whether Bon ever worked a stadium up as well as Brian does. Brian makes it look totally effortless.

The album and ensuing tour cemented AC/DC as a top-line rock band and live attraction. Even the previously unimpressed *Rolling Stone* in October 1980 reassessed the band in light of the spectacular success of the album and tour. What, they wondered, especially with their recent trauma, was their secret? 'We just get out there and rock', explained Angus. 'If your amp blows up, or your guitar packs it in, smash it up and pick up a new one. And that's how it always was with us'.

While all of the songs from *Back In Black* were played at least once on the tour, it became clear as the tour progressed which were the core songs on stage. These being 'Hells Bells', 'Shoot To Thrill', 'What Do You Do For Money Honey', 'Back In Black' and 'You Shook Me All Night Long'.

I was back to see them again at Birmingham Odeon in 1980. It was still AC/DC but it felt like a quite different version. There were props, too, along with Angus in a velvet suit! However, they were also, in the UK at least, still on the Odeon/Town Hall circuit, and they were clearly too big for that. You knew you were seeing a band who had gone up several notches and were a big draw, far too big now for that circuit. That they made it without Bon is a great shame, but Brian was the right man at the right time. He took his chance and never let go.

For Those About To Rock (1981)

Personnel:
Brian Johnson: lead vocals
Angus Young: lead guitar
Malcolm Young: rhythm guitar, backing vocals
Phil Rudd: drums
Robert John 'Mutt' Lange: backing vocals
Cliff Williams: bass, backing vocals
Produced by Robert John 'Mutt' Lange at Mobile One and H.I.S. in Paris, Family
Studio in Paris and Battery Studios in London between May and September 1981
Release date: 20 November 1981
Label: Albert/Atlantic
Highest chart places: Australia: 3, UK: 3, USA: 1
Running time: 40:10
All songs by Angus Young, Malcolm Young and Brian Johnson

The question of how to follow *Back In Black* was solved by Atlantic USA,
who decided to release *Dirty Deeds* at last. Phil Carson was horrified,
feeling it would put a lid on future AC/DC album sales; he may have been
right because sales of the next 'Brian' album *For Those About To Rock* were
nowhere near as impressive as *Back In Black*.

Dave Thoener worked as the mixing engineer on the sessions. He recalls
how he got involved:

I was at Long View Farms recording in North Brookfield, Massachusetts.
I was working on *Freeze Frame* by the J. Geils Band. Mutt called on the
studio line, asking if I was around. We were doing overdubs, so I paused
and took the call. Mutt said his favourite record the previous year was *Love
Stinks* (also by the J. Geils Band) and he asked if I'd be interested in coming
to Paris to finish recording with AC/DC. I told him I had another month
of work on Geils; in reality, I think it was another 6-7 weeks, including
mixing, which took a month alone. I checked with Seth Justman, who was
producing *Freeze Frame*, to ask if he thought we'd be done and told him the
opportunity. He said we'd be finished, so I committed, and my manager and
the band's manager worked out the details, pay, flight, per diem and hotel. I
finished *Freeze Frame* on a Saturday night, slept Sunday and got a flight to
Paris on Monday morning.

Thoener found that...

...Mark Dearnley had recorded the drums and bass in an empty stone
rehearsal studio with a remote truck named Mobile 1 out of England. So
my first day was recording rhythm guitars, then lead guitars. The lead
guitar solos were an overdub because the leakage would have been picked

up by the drum mics. Malcolm and Angus had two Marshall guitar amps daisy changed, so the amps were very loud. Mutt would have me put the Neumann U-87 capsule very close to the speaker cloth, thereby getting a proximity effect. I think we had one U-87 on each speaker and we would listen on the truck and decide which combination of microphones captured what he wanted. Up to that point in my career, I had never used mics on a guitar amp like that. But I used that trick many times after that experience. When I wanted a thick, in-your-face sound, that did the trick.

Angus would come into the truck and we had a stool for him to sit on and record his solos. Recording in a remote truck is a little claustrophobic. Mutt would be on one side of the console and I'd scoot over as much as I could to the other side so Angus could sit between the speakers and play against the rhythm mix we would put together. We'd run a cable from the truck to the amp in the stone room. Mutt would give him a little direction and then we'd watch the magic happen. Several solos would be recorded and then Mutt would either pick one in its entirety or put one together from a few bars here and there. Mutt is a genius – there's no other way to put it – as both a songwriter and a performer. He had everything planned out in his mind, which sometimes made it difficult for the musician to do. He'd concentrate for take after take until the performance was exactly what he wanted.

Thoener enjoyed his time with the Youngs: 'Malcolm was a wonderful person and we hung out a bit where the band was staying. He was very humble, friendly and funny. Angus was a bit more reserved'. With the guitar tracks recorded, they moved to Family Studios (also in Paris), where Brian's lead vocals were recorded. Thoener says that 'Brian was funny and friendly and he gave 100% every time. Sometimes, Mutt would want a certain phrase sung in a specific way. Brian would sing the phrase or word over and over until he sang it exactly as Mutt wanted'. Vocals recorded, the next and final stop was at Battery Studios (London) to mix the album. Thoener found the process to be more detailed and lengthy than expected:

Present at Battery Studios were just me and my assistant Nigel Green and Mutt. It was a 24-track mix and the first mix of the album. We did it in a day, and Mutt wanted to leave it up for a second day to check the mix the next morning when we were fresh. Since it was the first mix, it was extremely hard for Mutt to let go. The first mix shapes the sound of every mix that follows. That mix took five days before Mutt was ready to move on.

I thought to myself, 'Why is this decision taking so long?' I'm not one who focuses on that kind of detail. The big picture was always my concern. Once everything is up and close, I'll fine-tune a specific instrument because I know what that instrument is competing with, frequency-wise. Mutt insisted on making those decisions on each mix and then going forward. It was very time-consuming. We spent a month mixing the songs and out of 30 working days, we took off two.

The cover package is a mixed delight. Broadly speaking, the same package design was used across the world. The cannon on a gold background design is a strong motif emphasising the strength and success of the band. The gatefold picture of the band on stage has an immediate impact, but in truth, it's not a great picture. The back cover is similar in style to *Back In Black*, being predominately track titles. In Spain, they reversed the colours so that the cannon and lettering is gold on black. This makes for a continuity from *Back In Black* that arguably works even better.

The title of the album is strong, linking right to the best track. It's fair to say the album isn't as good as *Back In Black*, but that was near impossible. You could argue the band had toured heavily and had little time to prepare new material. But then, against that, they had even less time for *Back In Black* in far worse circumstances. After they finished touring *Back In Black* at the end of February 1981, they had two months spare before the five-month sojourn making the album. That's still not enough time to write quality material when, presumably, all concerned were blasted from the heavy touring. But what we get is a more than worthy album that contains three great songs in 'For Those About To Rock', 'C.O.D'. and the criminally underrated 'Spellbound'. However, a few of the tracks could have been a lot better. That being said, when fans discuss which is the best Brian album after *Back In Black*, this must be the biggest contender.

What Atlantic would have hoped for is a big-selling single or two to give the sales a nudge, but the album just doesn't have much in that way. 'Let's Get It Up', in fairness, somehow went Top Ten in America!

'For Those About To Rock (We Salute You)'
Angus's inspiration came from a book he was reading about gladiators. This is likely to be Daniel Mannix's 1958 book *Those About To Die*, which was in print for three decades and was the basis of the Ridley Scott film *Gladiator*.

From the first notes, this is epic; the intro is simply outstanding and grabs you every time you hear it. The catchy doubled stuttering riff stands alone until Phil and Malcolm come in for support. One issue with the intro is Brian or what to do with him. He comes in at 49 seconds and basically wails and groans until he enters fully after Rudd's turnaround at 1:19. I feel they should have held him back completely till 1:19 because what he does before that is of little consequence. The cannon sounds are an intrinsic part, but nobody has ever said where they were recorded. Dave Thoener isn't telling, either. 'It's a trade secret. I've read many comments as to what people believe generated that sound, but no one has ever, or will ever, guess how it was created'.

Going back to listen to the studio original after hearing so many live versions is quite a shock. The slow and deliberate intro is a stark contrast to the full-on attack and assault of the live versions. The studio version comes out best because of the better definition of the riff.

We are used to it being used at the end of the set live, understandably so, as this is a monumental set closer. Here, they open the album with it and it works just as brilliantly, although it does prove hard to follow!

After the understated early half of the song, the switch begins at 2:45 with Angus's solo, which ups the pressure levels and Brian and the band audibly 'react' to that at 3:17 – 'We're just a battery for hire with a guitar fire'. It's all more intense and the first cannon blast at 3:35 heralds the long outro with everything at full blast - guitars, bass, drums, Brian, backing vocals and the cannons! It really is an astonishingly visceral ending. See them play it live and it never fails to get to you, but it all started here. It was released as the second single from the album.

'Put The Finger On You'
This has the almost impossible task of trying to follow that classic opener. It's quite basic in approach and they don't sell the chorus particularly well. It's all too repetitive, veering on being tiresome! Everything in the song works as it should, but it sounds too routine and (whisper it) a bit lifeless. Nothing about it says 'classic 'or 'excellent' or even 'very good'. It would have been better bumped down the tracklist, more hidden in the running order. Here, it's too exposed as a weaker track following the bombastic opener. A better choice here would have been 'C.O.D'.

'Let's Get It Up'
Lyrically, this has no subtle touches. It's a full-on sexual metaphor song that sadly misses its punches. The problem, from a fan's point of view, is that it's all rather lazy. The best parts of the song are the fills and riffs before the chorus, as can be heard first at 0:48. There's a tautness and musicality there that brightens the song due to the dull-sounding main riff. Even Phil sounds like he's not sure about this one! It all relies on the chorus delivering, but it doesn't. In mitigation, Angus's solo is good! And finally, this was never a good choice for the first, or indeed, any single!

'Inject The Venom'
The hammer-down, biting intro is most welcome after the sluggishness of 'Let's Get It Up'. Brian audibly enjoys his rambunctious intro vocals – so far, so good. The verses still lean on that intro riff, but it's the chorus where things get much more interesting. The gang vocals are accompanied by a different riff. It's catchy and a real earworm. Angus's solo (2:03) is the high point, as his guitar snarls and bends around Malcolm's riff and a splendid drum part from Phil. From there, they wisely stick to repeating the chorus till the outro. This is not a great track, but the chorus and solo section do enough to make the song a keeper.

'Snowballed'

This gets somewhere close to the back-to-basics approach the band would adopt on *Flick Of The Switch*. Without a big chorus, the verses lose momentum. Brian is audibly energised by it, though. Quite what being 'snowballed' means is open to question. Some have suggested cocaine, which, allegedly, was being used by the band at this time. However, in Brian's lyrical mind, snowballed is slang for getting shafted in a variety of situations. They all sound bad enough – but 'snowballed', no, I don't get it at all! The music is punchy and crisp, with real attitude and push, especially on the verses, but in the end, this is a rather confused track that could have been so much better.

'Evil Walks'

The evil walking 'beside you' is a 'black widow weaving evil notions'. The slow intro with the guitars and cymbals is great, a classic build-up. The main body of the song is a burning groove with plenty of room for the song to breathe. The guitar melody line acts as a connector between Brian and the rhythm track. The chorus doesn't deviate greatly from the verses; there's not enough of a lift to it, which is a shame. They could have boosted it more. The section at 2:37 after the solo, where they take it down, is excellent. They're back into the blues here, so Brian instantly feels right at home, while Angus mirrors his pain with some lovely wailing lead lines. The outro is one long chorus, with Angus firing off another great solo for good measure. There's enough here to make this worth its place on the album, but it could have been better.

'C. O. D'.

Another one that holds its own with the best of *Back In Black*, this is a fabulous song. An absolutely killer groove from Cliff and Phil suckers you in. This is a rhythm section, and the band are absolutely on top of their game! The way Phil has that slight drag on the rhythm works brilliantly with the riff.

Lyrically, it's one of their best songs in the Brian years, with some interesting choices as to the 'C.O.D.' – 'care of the devil, cash on demand' etc. Brian audibly has a ball with the lyrics. The backing vocals are well done, too, with an insistent edge to them that hammers the choruses home. I could listen to this on repeat for ages for the feel and groove and the squalling lead lines from Angus. C.O.D. - class on delivery!

'Breaking The Rules'

It's a filler track which never seems to quite get going. The intro hints at a promise of better things, but it all backs off with the inoffensive lick that comes in at the 30-second mark. And this is the core of the problem; a song called 'Breaking The Rules' should be wild and untamed and this just isn't that at all. The chorus is big but inoffensive when it needed plenty of attitude.

'Night Of The Long Knives'

This is another one that needed something special added to it. It's odd because the title, at least, is inspired by the events in 1934 in Germany when the Nazis consolidated their power. Lyrically, it looks like it might be linked to that, but only in a vague way and understandably so. The chorus is hopeless, being nothing more than the title chanted at a curiously high pitch – it just doesn't deliver. There's a snaking riff that isn't bad, but that's the best of the song, really.

'Spellbound'

Things were getting a bit dull there on the running order, but they save it with this great closing song. It's a deep, moody, brooding track, confirmed by the lyrics, which sees the band touching on life at its numbing worst. Brian's 'situation' sounds hopeless, or 'spellbound, my world keeps tumbling down'. This is unusually despondent for AC/DC, it has to be said; a surprise lyric from a band who you would think were on top of the world. Yet, it sounds like it comes from a personal experience; Brian is quite convincing.

What the song also does is connect with any fans who might be going through bad times. Some may well have found reassurance that they are not alone. From the Bon era, you could draw a parallel with 'Down Payment Blues', but that has a humour to it that 'Spellbound' simply doesn't. It hasn't got the same instant appeal as the equally sombre 'Hells Bells' either. But the mournful riff with the tight rhythm track is a treat, and Angus cracks off a stunning solo, which he seems to have been saving up for a while on this album. It's almost like they know they need to go out in style. Crank this one up; there's a mighty beast here waiting to be rediscovered.

Flick Of The Switch (1983)

Personnel:
Brian Johnson: lead vocals
Angus Young: lead guitar
Malcolm Young: rhythm guitar, backing vocals
Cliff Williams: bass, backing vocals
Phil Rudd: drums
Produced by Malcolm and Angus Young at Compass Point Studios, Nassau,
between April and May 1983. Vocals re-recorded by George Young, and final
mix, at Electric Lady Studios, New York, May 1983.
Release date: 19 August 1983
Label: Albert/Atlantic
Highest chart places: Australia: 3, UK: 4, USA: 15
Running time: 37:02
All songs by Angus Young, Malcolm Young and Brian Johnson

Mutt Lange was gone, and after the big production feel of the previous three
albums, *Flick Of The Switch* saw the band return to a more basic approach,
more how they saw themselves. Angus told *Guitar World* in 1984 that 'we
wanted this one as raw as possible. We wanted a natural but big sound for
the guitars. We didn't want echoes and reverb going everywhere and noise
eliminators and noise extractors'.

Electric Lady was booked for final mixing and George Young was invited
in to listen and comment. Engineer Barry Harris told the *Highway To AC/DC*
website that ...

...this is where, for me, the process changed. They decided to scrap all the
vocals and fine-tune the lyrics. So, while Tony (Platt) was working in Studio
A, I went to Studio B with George and Brian to record new vocals. Brian
rewrote some lyrics on the spot and then George helped him get his best
performance down on tape.

It was a good decision because George got some great performances out of
Brian and it showcases him at his best. The lyrics that needed replacing raise
eyebrows – how bad must they have been?! You also have to wonder how the
album might have sounded with Vanda and Young producing it.

As a further response to the Lange-era productions, the album was all
finished in about a month. The sonic changes were welcomed by some
hardcore fans, but it might have been a different proposition for those who
came on board with the Mutt Lange albums. Possibly hard for them to digest
at first, if ever. The dilemma for AC/DC was that they had reached a plateau
with Lange. Once there, where do you go that equals it? *Flick Of The Switch*
looked to some like a backward step, and that's a shame because there is a
lot to enjoy on the album.

The consequent drop-off in sales made this the poorest-selling album since *Powerage*. There were three key problems. Firstly, the back-to-basics philosophy was picked up by the drab album cover by Brent Richardson, an utterly nondescript line drawing of Angus about to flick the switch. As first impressions go, this was a bad mistake. Secondly, there was the lack of any radio-friendly 'hits', and thirdly, there was the less glossy, more raw production. Some have said the songs were not quite up to scratch either, but they are often as good as those on *For Those About To Rock*. You can easily hear, though, how Lange could have polished them up into more radio-friendly big songs. But they are raw and exciting, too. I am one of those who likes the sparse, no-frills production.

On the personnel front, Phil's increasing issues saw a huge fallout with Malcolm, which soon led to his dismissal from the band. Barry Harris doesn't list Phil as being among those present for the Electric Lady mixing/recording sessions. But it is generally accepted, and confirmed by Barry Harris, that Phil completed all the drum parts. However, it's also known that former Procol Harum drummer Barrie James (aka 'B. J'.) Wilson was flown out to the studios. Every official source always says Phil Rudd's tracks are intact on the album, but there is a possibility that Wilson recorded the two outtakes from later in the sessions. Whatever went down, the loss of Phil Rudd was a critical blow to the band's sound.

'Rising Power'

A great 'start as you mean to go on' intro greets us as the band hammer into the swaggering catchy-as-hell riff. It's married to an insistent groove, and it all goes up several notches with a great vocal from Brian. He is on terrific form, delivering the lyrics with real excitement and, well, yes, rising power! The boys show what they learned from Lange with the big backing vocals on the choruses. As choruses go, it's up there with their best work in the Brian era, a full rabble-rousing, fist-in-the-air sing-along focussing on the two words of the title. Angus's solo is interesting. He plays a lovely subtle melody around the riff before unleashing some more ferocious typical Angus solo guitar. It's relatively short and sweet, but he does come back for more in the outro, where he lets rip again.

Although the song is not generally highly rated, its 'electric snap and crackle' was, and is, an attention grabber. It's an excellent song.

'This House Is On Fire'

The power and intent left in your head from 'Rising Power' is maintained. The sheer weight of the opening riff, with one rhythm guitar joined by a second, is uncompromising. Brian gets things moving with a just about intelligible 'Yonder she walks' and a yelp, and then in comes the rhythm track. Phil's drumming is 'the rudder 'at his best; he just drives this along. His cymbal crashes in the first 30 seconds, adding so much colour. The gang vocal chorus is strong; the backing vocals are always more tuneful post-Lange. The chorus riff works well with the melody line. There's a middle eight at 2:01, a gear shift in the vocals and rhythm leading right into Angus's solo. He's a little low in the mix for the first bars, but he then soars out with a solo that uses the melody line for inspiration. He returns to it for the outro, which would be a bit laboured, but for his fills, which keep your attention.

A big grandstand end finishes it off nicely. It's generally one of the better-rated tracks on the album.

'Flick Of The Switch'
Phil counts in on his hi-hat and the band crash in for a high-tempo groove with a nice twisting riff. Brian is a bit too low in the mix, which he often is on this album. The chorus is nice and strong, a real sing-along effort, but the mix is a bit off here, too, with the backing vocals too low. The song is a bit pedestrian and only really takes off when Angus's solo comes in at 1:48. This is not one of his best efforts, though it could be that there's just too much riding on it. He gets to run riot over the outro with guitar fills, which do a lot to keep interest levels up. This song is average at best, although Atlantic liked it enough to make it the third single in America.

'Nervous Shakedown'
It's easily one of the best songs on the album right from the opening bars – even if they aren't far off 'Rising Power' again. The stop-start riff apes 'Back In Black' in part as well, but this one has its own nuggets of gold in a killer chorus and a fret-melting solo from Angus. The song has a hard-edged swagger and swing that represents AC/DC at their best, and it's one that justifies their decision to keep things raw. But you can imagine how Lange would have polished this up to *Back In Black* levels. The chorus is good enough, but he would have taken the backing vocals to another level. It was picked out to be the second single from the album.

'Landslide'
The performance of this fast boogie shuffle has spirit, but overall, it just lacks that something to make it a great song. Even the solo doesn't really brighten things up; in the end, this is average filler in spite of their enthusiasm. It just isn't memorable.

'Guns For Hire'
Angus gets to imitate gunshots for the second time (after 'Jailbreak') on the jagged, staccato intro. The song doesn't quite hit the mark after that peak, mostly down to the rather dull chorus. The verses are a bit routine as well. It was picked out as the debut single from the album, but it lacked that extra spark to be a commercial hit.

'Deep In The Hole'

A strong, direct and (very) basic tune. They don't get it out of the mid-tempo plod that holds it down and there's little of interest. The chorus is way too dull and repetitive, almost brainwashing in its nursery rhyme simplicity. This one should have been replaced or dramatically livened up.

'Bedlam In Belgium'

Lyrically, this was apparently inspired by a ruck between fans and the police at a concert at Dancing Thierbrau in Kontich, Belgium, on 9 October 1977. So, one imagines Brian did not write all the lyrics to this one! In fact, these are some of the best lyrics on the album by far, with more effort put in. It has a great feel in the rhythm and the pacing is good. The chorus works well, which is a bit of a surprise, given the cumbersome title! It sounds like it's all going to end at 2:46 with the band coming together for a crescendo, but no, they go for a minute more with choruses all the way to the outro. A good song that is worth its place on the album.

'Badlands'

With an addictive groove, this is easily one of the best songs on the album, being a raw and exciting powerhouse that just keeps giving. The transition from verse to chorus is brilliant and so smooth. Brian holds off for a moment on his first line in each chorus, the pause giving extra weight to the words. He gives the song a really personal vibe as he recounts his story. The song has some Led Zeppelin overtones to it; the guitars remind me of Jimmy Page's slide work on 'In My Time Of Dying'.

'Brain Shake'

It's not a great finish to the album. It's a steamroller of a song, but other than the pace, there's not enough else to justify it. The chorus is one of the most mundane they ever recorded, topping even 'Deep In The Hole' for sheer monotony, though Brian (bless him) tries his best to give it some oomph! Another one that didn't deserve to make the cut.

Outtakes

There are two reported outtakes, 'Tightrope' and 'Out Of Bounds', neither of which have surfaced on the Internet.

What Happened Next?

With a tour due, the band auditioned for a new drummer in May/June 1983 using a soundstage in New York. Among those who are said to have auditioned were Simon Kirke (Free/ Bad Company), Denny Carmassi (Montrose) and Brian's old mate Paul Thompson (Roxy Music). He recalled his audition to *Classic Rock* in December 2023: 'Brian Johnson, who I'd grown up with back in the Geordie days, rang up and said they were looking for drummers and to expect a call from their tour manager. He called the next day and invited me to go over to New York, where the band were finishing their Flick Of The Switch album, and have a try-out for a few days. And he gave me a few AC/DC songs to learn – 'Back In Black', 'Shot Down In Flames' and 'Highway To Hell".

I flew over and joined them at the Parker Meridien Hotel. The first evening, I went down to the rehearsal studios at SIR, where they had a drum kit set up and I spent a couple of hours setting it up my way and playing around a bit. The next day, I went with Angus, Malcolm and Cliff and we tried out the songs. I remember the room was set up like a tiny club with this little stage and a mixer at the other end of the room where one of the crew was recording it onto cassette. At the end, they asked if I could learn a few more songs and come back and try them tomorrow. We spent several days playing more songs in the studio. Everything seemed to be going well from my point of view. I felt I was playing okay and I was also getting on with them well. It was obvious to me that Malcolm and Angus were in control, but I really admired what they were doing. They did it their way and they didn't compromise'.

But Thompson was passed over, and in the end, they went for 19-year-old Simon Wright. Barry Harris recalls them turning up with Simon during the Electric Lady sessions. Simon (born 19 June 1963, Oldham) was a new name to many, but he had recorded in Britain with New Wave of British Heavy Metal bands A II Z and Tytan. Simon recalled what happened to *VWMusic* in 2021:

I was really shocked when I went for the audition. I had no idea it was AC/DC. I didn't even know they were looking for a drummer, to be honest with you. I was just playing with the drum tech, did the audition, went back and then I met the band. They were just really down-to-earth and so un-starish. I moved into a new apartment, then I had money, but I didn't have any big plans or anything because I was so young. I just wanted to play; I wanted to do a gig with this band, learn all the songs and rehearse. I knew a lot of the songs from the past because I loved AC/DC. It was a bit of a whirlwind, but they were cool and pretty grounded.

The obvious issue for Simon was replacing Phil Rudd:

When I got the gig, I thought to myself, 'Well, okay, that's the music. That's the way. That's the formula with Phil', it's pretty straightforward; you can't really jump all over that. I just pretty much copied what Phil had done. It was a bit baffling at first with some of the songs. I hadn't realised it, but with Phil's playing, it's the bedrock. AC/DC is all about the swing of the song, the groove and stuff, which is Phil. I tried to do my best to emulate Phil with total respect.

93

The setlist for the tour didn't show much confidence in the album, with only 'Guns For Hire' (the usual opening song) and the title track regularly appearing. It was also a noticeably shorter tour than normal, with a near eight-month gap between the North American and European dates.

'74 Jailbreak (Atlantic)

1984 would have been a year without a new album, but Atlantic saw an opportunity. They still had some unreleased songs in America in the vaults. Thus, the curiously cobbled-together *'74 Jailbreak* EP came to be released on 10 October 1984. To be clear on this, there is nothing wrong with the tracks; it's the presentation and nature of the release that is plain wrong.

To a casual browser, it wasn't obvious that these were 'archive' tracks or that every track featured Bon and was originally rejected by Atlantic USA. The selection itself was made up of four internationally unreleased tracks from their debut album ('You Ain't Got A Hold On Me', 'Show Business', 'Soul Stripper' and 'Baby Please Don't Go'), plus 'Jailbreak', that had bafflingly not made the eventual USA *Dirty Deeds* release.

The EP left 'Stick Around', 'School Days' and 'Love Song' still awaiting international release and it's crazy that Atlantic didn't use this opportunity to tie up loose ends. All three of the 'missing' tracks could easily have been added, albeit that 'Love Song' is a candidate for their poorest song!

The cash-in cheap feel of the release is compounded by the cover, which is a stage shot of Angus repeated several times and staggered to imply movement.

Fly On The Wall (1985)

Personnel:
Brian Johnson: lead vocals
Angus Young: lead guitar
Malcolm Young: rhythm guitar, backing vocals
Cliff Williams: bass, backing vocals
Simon Wright: drums
Produced by Malcolm and Angus Young at Mountain Studios, Montreux,
between October 1984 and February 1985
Release date: 28 June 1985
Label: Albert/Atlantic
Highest chart places: Australia: 4, UK: 7, USA: 32
Running time: 40:30
All songs by Angus Young, Malcolm Young and Brian Johnson

Flick Of The Switch had seen Malcolm and Angus deliver a grittier production
that nodded back towards the pre-Lange era. For *Fly On The Wall*, they took
it several stages further away from the gloss. Mountain Studios was new to
them and something went wrong because the production does the band few
favours. It had all looked promising at first, with the band sending engineer
Mark Dearnley to check the studio out. Uniquely, the studio makes use of a
large octagonal room, part of the Montreux casino, which is used for the Jazz
Festivals. Dearnley enthused about the room in *Home And Studio Recording*
in 1985, further singling out Angus' solos in the studio for special mention:

It is an enormous, superb live room, ideal for a good rock 'n' roll band who
can play together at once. After working with drum machines and all those
things, it is great to be able to forget about machinery and click tracks.
...the backing tracks were recorded with the whole band playing
together, guitar solos and vocals being overdubbed afterwards, along
with one or two bits of reinforcement on the guitar parts, and practically
nothing on the backing tracks was replaced. It is all down to feel. The
band enjoy playing together as a band and they do it very well, so they get
the best feel that way
Angus had a Schaeffer radio pickup, which he uses on stage, so he
used that playing in the control room, using the hall as ambience with the
speakers wired up downstairs. We ended up with a very complicated sound
due to the nature of the radio microphone – it was a very interesting sound.

Dearnley also noted that special care was taken with Brian's vocals. 'On
previous albums, working with other producers, it was more usual to record
all the backing tracks and then overdub. This time, however, they decided
to work on two tracks at a time, giving Brian's lead vocal a chance to
breathe'. In spite of the care shown to him, Brian, in particular, comes off

badly in the mix, sounding distant and unintelligible on most of the tracks. The touring schedule, even with breaks, must have been a factor in his diminishing vocal power. Meanwhile, poor Simon Wright's drums are treated with heavy reverb.

The cover, by Todd Schorr, is dreadful, a cartoon based on an uninspired title that flies in the face of the band's arena-filling stature. It doesn't even work as a piece of descriptive art – there is no wall - it's a fence!

Along with the low-fi production and a paucity of great songs, what is evidently missing too is the groove and swagger that you hear in so much of their best material. This could have been a better album with an outside producer getting more from the songs and a better mix. The best of an often mediocre bunch are 'Sink The Pink' and 'Shake Your Foundations'.

'Fly On The Wall'

The intro is promising enough. Simon comes in crisply and doesn't let the side down. The chorus is strong, too, and is only let down by the shockingly poor vocal mix (a regular theme). In fact, the instrument mix is off, too, with a distracting reverb-heavy muddiness. That's a shame because the song itself sounds good; you can imagine what it *could* have been if we could hear it properly. Malcolm is cranking out a strong rhythm part in there, for instance. On the whole, this is a frustratingly painful listen.

'Shake Your Foundations'

This was released as the third single, and in spite of the production and lack of gloss, it got to number 24 in the UK chart! Simon is great in the intro, especially the way he hangs off the beat. That intro leads into a blaster of a guitar riff. Brian's vocals are commanding as he stamps his personality all over the song in spite of being too low in the mix! The chorus has a nursery rhyme-like repeat of 'aye aye oh, shake your foundations', but they deliver it with such gusto that, to an extent, it works. This is one of the stronger songs on the album and is even better on *Who Made Who*, where George Young remixes it. If only he had been asked to remix the whole album.

'First Blood'

You can hear exactly what this album could have been in the intro. Angus and Malcolm's tight interplay is as convincing as ever but lost in the thin production. Angus's solo is effective, but the rhythm section aren't at their best; this is one where they obviously miss Phil. The main trouble is the weakness of the composition itself, though the chorus shows some teeth and attitude.

'Danger'

The sawing slow riff and steadier tempo initially makes for a welcome change of pace on the album. The laid-back groove is a relief, as is being able to hear

Brian properly. However much the rhythm riff appeals, it means that Simon is reduced to a basic plod that does him little favours. Lyrically, it's poor stuff and the chorus is uninteresting and repetitive, even by their standards! It was the first single released from the album and crept into the UK Top 50 at number 48.

'Sink The Pink'
I like to imagine that the title came from a game of snooker, but the phrase takes on quite a different meaning here! This is the best track on the album, a real crash, bang, wallop of a song. It's all there in the classic intro with Angus's gnarly guitar and Simon swinging it in style. Brian is reasonably audible and he holds his own over the powerhouse backing track, complete with heavily reverbed drums! The chorus delivers prime AC/DC with gang-backing vocals.

It was the second single from the album but failed to chart anywhere.

'Playing With Girls'
A sledgehammer beat adorns this average, soupy-sounding song. The lack of distinction in the mix lets it all down. Equally, Brian is largely unintelligible. The riff is energetic, as is Angus's solo, but that's the best of it. It's not a song to come back to often!

'Stand Up'
One of the better tracks, helped by being the best-sounding track sonically on the album by far. Suddenly, Brian is completely audible and there is a warmth and presence in the music that we haven't had anywhere else on the album. It has a real anthemic feel to it, especially in the big sing-along chorus. The riff has a catchy, sinuous, twisting feel to it that appeals, while Angus tears off a shrieking, wild solo that takes the song right over the edge. If only the whole album was like this.

'Hell Or High Water'
Angus's 'Won't Get Fooled Again' style guitar stands out on the intro, albeit it all sounds similar to the intro in 'Fly On The Wall' at a different tempo. There is a sparkle to the song that raises the pulse, especially the slashing guitar on the chorus with the Mutt Lange-style fist-pumping vocals. On the negatives, Brian is too low and the song loses its way after the intro. It's good, but it could have been a lot better.

'Back In Business'
Another of the best tracks. It has a dirty, fulsome riff with ZZ Top overtones. There's not much more to it than that, other than a gang vocal chorus, which is little more than the repeated title. Angus's solo draws from ZZ Top as well. The riff and the energy are enough to make this a keeper. Brian is pretty audible, too, which always helps!

'Send For The Man'

The brutal sledgehammer riff is a cracker, especially when the Youngs play it together. Brian is fairly incomprehensible save for the chorus but is audibly giving it his all. A great solo from Angus fires it up, maybe his best on the album. However, Simon's drums are little more than a slow stomp that does nothing for the song at all. This is a very good finish to the album, perhaps artificially so because of the paucity of top-drawer songs, but at least it ends with some verve and bite.

Blow Up Your Video (1988)

Personnel:
Brian Johnson: lead vocals
Angus Young: lead guitar
Malcolm Young: rhythm guitar, backing vocals
Cliff Williams: bass, backing vocals
Simon Wright: drums
Produced by Harry Vanda and George Young at Miraval Studios, Correns,
between August and September 1987
Release date: 29 January 1988
Label: Albert/Atlantic
Highest chart places: Australia: 2, UK: 2, USA: 12
Running time: 42:48
All songs by Angus Young, Malcolm Young and Brian Johnson

The return of Harry and George was a relief for the band. Both knew what
the band wanted to get across. Angus recalled to the *Auckland Star* in 1990
that it was 'great to turn around and say, 'Excuse me, I'm just gonna play a
bit of rock music here'. It was the best thing we've recorded for a while; we
just ignored the influence of the record company and any producers'. The
title, said Angus to *MTV Australia* in 1988, was a reaction against prevailing
trends:

> We were always a band that were best seen in a live situation and that's how
> the title came about. It's not to be taken like go out and blow up your video.
> Everything's automatic these days; a kid can go and flick on a button and get
> it coming in from all over the world.

Great sentiments, but it's still a terrible title. Far better to have gone with
'Heatseeker', which would have linked with the best track and inspired a
better cover. Angus bursting out of a video through a TV screen was fine for
the times but has dated badly.

Musically, it's a mixed bag of an album. 'Heatseeker' is superb and 'That's
The Way I Wanna Rock 'n' Roll' and 'Meanstreak' are excellent. There are
a few others that are very good, but sadly, also more than a few that are
average. It doesn't hit home with the punches in the way that it should. AC/
DC should never be bland, but this album comes dangerously close at times.

During the sessions, George Young noticed that Malcolm's drinking had
become a problem. 'I saw the signs', he told *Rolling Stone* in 2008. 'Malcolm
had a problem. I said if he didn't get his act together, I was out of there. I
don't recall it having any effect. In our family, if we have a problem, we deal
with it ourselves. There's no point in people telling us we gotta stop this or
that'. Nobody has stated that Malcolm's issues affected the recording of the
album, but George's comments must mean it was a slight hindrance at least.

While the album was spoken of in some sections of the press as a return to form, it was far from that. The band were capable of better material and more consistency. Harry and George are normally impeccable, but the production, too is flawed, a little bright and brash.

'Heatseeker'
An exciting, superb start to the album. If only they could have come up with an album's worth of material like this, it would have been as good as *Back In Black*. It comes out of the traps at full speed and has a melodic, almost poppy feel without losing the AC/DC raunch and swagger. The studio chatter in the intro enhances the live feel. The chords in the verses work brilliantly as a counterpoint to the continual surging riff. The understated chorus is one of their best, too; as minimal as it is lyrically, but it just hits the spot. Angus somehow squeezes in a brief solo that works with the song's melody. It's a sublimely well-judged piece of playing. It was wisely picked as the first single (backed with 'Go Zone').

'That's The Way I Wanna Rock 'n' Roll'
This effective song means the album has a really solid one-two-opening punch. It showcases Simon Wright at his best, although, in fairness to him, he's excellent on the entire album. There's a 50s rock 'n' roll feel to the intro with the guitar, cymbals and drums interplay. Brian picks up on this in the second verse (1:00), where he throws in some 50s song references and even name-checks The Wrecking Crew session musicians. The best part of the song is the solo, with Angus playing over that ubiquitous riff from Malcolm.

It was the second single, backed with 'Kissin' Dynamite' and the non-album 'Borrowed Time'.

'Meanstreak'
There are two rhythm parts – a sawing rhythm guitar and a more fluid walking riff. The combination of the two works a treat, with an almost funk feel to it. There's a great bit at just 43 seconds in when Brian sings 'But I ain't seen nothing to get me off my ass' with a unison backing vocal. It adds extra punch and emphasis. They repeat the effect later but not as effectively. The song features one of Angus's best solos on the album, as brief as it is. The spaces that Brian leaves between his phrasing allows the riff to pop up. Lyrically, it's decent enough and you have to laugh when they get playful in the lyrics. Part of the 'mean streak' is that 'I always kick the castle that's been built up on the beach', sings Brian. An excellent song, making three crackers in a row!

'Go Zone'
Back to basics for a real meat and potatoes song. However, while the riff is strong enough, the song doesn't have enough else of interest about it. The chorus is barely different to the verses, so there is no real sense of a lift or

dynamics. The best part is Angus's solo cued in with some tasty Townshend-like ('Won't Get Fooled Again') guitar at 2:37.

'Kissin' Dynamite'
A bluesy intro piques interest immediately. Simon's cymbal accents working in tandem with the guitar. When the band come slamming in with Brian's cry of 'Here she comes, here she comes', it sounds so powerful. Credit here again to Simon, who nails the Phil Rudd beat. Unfortunately, Brian sounds uncomfortable. If the key had been dropped, this would have suited him better, but as it is, he is on the edge of his comfort zone. There's still enough snap and power in the song to make it worthy, especially the seemingly relentless choruses – but it's no classic.

'Nick Of Time'
While nothing on the album is as good as the opening trio, this is one that could have joined them. The urgent intro, with the cymbals, fast bass and twin rhythm guitars, is purposeful, building up to the big riff. The riff is decent enough, but other than that, there's a lack of much else interesting going on. It all comes over as a bit pedestrian with a lack-lustre chorus.

'Some Sin For Nuthin"
A real challenger to the opening trio. This has a swagger, swing and sassiness to it that is irresistible. If Phil Rudd featured, this would have been even more of a contender. You can hear how he would have handled this. Simon just doesn't have Phil's feel. I love the droning solo from Angus, followed by a bluesy outpouring. This song has sadly become forgotten over the years.

'Ruff Stuff'
The intro reminds me of 'Through The Mists Of Time' in a lower key. The wandering melody guitar line is nice, and Angus tears out a wild finger-tapping solo and some screaming licks. But it's not enough, although it's still a better-than-average song. It is surprisingly inoffensive, given the title!

'Two's Up'
We begin with the riff backed by a wall of noise rhythm section. The 'Shoot To Thrill'-style lick makes a welcome reappearance, always guaranteed to grab your attention. This is a well-crafted song that stands out in their catalogue and is worthy of more respect. It's almost a hair metal song in some ways. The chorus, in particular, is a punchy, pop-sounding affair. However, there's enough of the AC/DC stamp on this experiment to make it work well.

'This Means War'
As soon as the band hit the throttle, it's a berserk rush of noise that hits hard. Where it goes wrong is the uninteresting chorus, which adds nothing. Best

of all is the spiralling, fast riff, a real cracker which deserved a more suitable home. A disappointing final track, really.

Additional Songs

In addition to the following songs, three more are also known to exist. The *AC/DC Tours De France* book features a sheet list of songs from Studio Miraval that includes 'Reproduce', '13th' and 'Number's Up'. The latter is a different song to 'Two's Up' because both are listed on the sheet.

'Borrowed Time'

This should have been on the album because it's a better song than a few that made the cut. It can be found on the *Backtracks* compilation, but the intro is edited. The riff and the chorus could have done with a bit more beefing up but the potential is there. Angus certainly thought so because he cracks off a great solo. Instead of being polished up, the song was left as it was and crept out first on the 'That's The Way I Wanna Rock 'N' Roll' single.

'Down On The Borderline'

This was later released on the Australian 'Moneytalks' single, which means it was, in effect, rejected for two albums. That's a shame because this high-quality song really should have been featured on either *Blow Up* or *Razor's Edge*. The stuttering main riff, for example, is naggingly catchy and deserved to be attached to a more widely familiar AC/DC song. The rhythm is rock solid, vintage AC/DC. The chorus hits it home, with Malcolm and Cliff on backing vocals. All this and a tasty guitar solo as well! So why was it not thought better of by the band? Perhaps it was just felt to be 'too different'. Hear this excellent song also on *Backtracks*.

'Snake Eye'

This first appeared on the 'Heatseeker' single. It found its rightful home as a B-side, being filler all the way. They hang onto the monotonous riff for dear life and there's nothing happening elsewhere to lift the mood. It's another one you can find on *Backtracks*.

'Alright Tonight'

Not officially released, but it's available on YouTube in a rough-sounding rehearsal form. The almost funky riff is fabulous; this is a track that could have added some variety to the album without losing the AC/DC vibe. Angus's solo is a complete contrast to the song's melody and not a great fit in truth, but otherwise, this is well worth checking out.

'Let It Loose'

This is another officially unreleased one available on YouTube. It's similarly rough to 'Alright Tonight' but doesn't have the spark which that song has. It hangs upon a riff that doesn't especially stand out, so they wisely canned it.

What Happened Next?

Malcolm managed the first two legs of the supporting tour, which visited Australia and Europe. But when the band took the stage for the first American date on 3 May 1988 at Portland, Malcolm was not there. In his place was Stevie Young, Malcolm and Angus's nephew and the son of their elder brother Stephen Young. Simon Wright explained to *VWMusic* in 2021 what happened:

We started touring and everything seemed fine. About halfway through, Malcolm started drinking. He had problems at home with his son and stuff, all these health issues – it was awful. We did one show, I think it was in France in an open-air place, and Malcolm got really drunk. I've never seen him get drunk on stage, but he was hanging off the cymbal stands and trying to pull them over – it was bizarre. So, we managed to get through that gig and we all walked to the edge of the stage, and at the bottom of the steps going down, Malcolm and (not named) were in fisticuffs at the bottom, just balls of legs and arms going off. So, we had to sit down and talk and Mal was really upset about things. He had to stop being on the road and go home. Thankfully, he got better and he got his son doing fine again. In the interim, Stevie (Young) came in and he just slid right in. Stevie plays a lot like Mal. He knew what the gig needed. He came in and was a great guy and did a fantastic, brilliant job. Stevie left everything out there when we needed him.

Malcolm would not return to the stage until the *Razor's Edge* tour two years later. This was the final tour for Simon Wright, who left at the end of it, seeking new challenges and opportunities with Dio. Wright's reason for leaving, said Angus to *Auckland Star* in 1990, was because he 'got itchy feet. He felt he wanted to be doing more'.

Simon never gets the credit he deserves for his work with the band. He never let them down and his playing was always what they wanted. But for the most part, he was no Phil Rudd, who is 'the man' when it comes to drumming for AC/DC. That's just how it is.

The Razor's Edge (1990)
Personnel:
Brian Johnson: lead vocals
Angus Young: lead guitar
Malcolm Young: rhythm guitar, backing vocals
Cliff Williams: bass, backing vocals
Chris Slade: drums
Produced by Bruce Fairbairn at Windmill Lane Studios, Dublin, and Little
Mountain Sound, Vancouver, 1990
Release date: 24 September 1990
Label: Albert/Atco
Highest chart places: Australia: 3, UK: 4, USA: 2
Running time: 46:11
All songs by Angus and Malcolm Young

Angus explained to Martin Aston to *Auckland Star* in 1990 that 'We wanted a title that sounded tough, to cut the bullshit because that's what we are, in our music, though not as people. We aren't Mike Tysons!' That philosophy went through into the songs they recorded with new producer Bruce Fairbairn. Angus was impressed by Fairbairn's approach: 'When I sit on that side of the world, I always think producers are going to be high-powered, you know, more business than pleasure. But Bruce was really good. I was shocked in a way because the guy said, 'I want you to sound like AC/DC when you were 17'.' Fairbairn was, in fact, the replacement producer along with his engineer/ mixer Mike Fraser. Fraser recalls how they came in:

Razors Edge was recorded at Windmill Lane with George Young. About halfway through, there was a family emergency or something and George couldn't finish the record. The band reached out to Bruce (Fairbairn) and asked if he could finish the record off for them. At the time, Bruce and I were working a lot together. Bruce always worked in Vancouver when possible, so the band came out here to finish the recordings. All we were supposed to do was record lead vocals and guitar solos. On one of the first songs we started to do vocals, we had to change the key, which required us to rerecord the bass and guitars. The boys liked the sound of the new guitars, so we ended up redoing all the rest of the songs.

While the media may have thought AC/DC were churning out another album, there was, according to Angus, a key difference this time in the way the songs were constructed. He told the *Auckland Star* in 1990 that 'instead of being riff-makers all the time and thinking we could make tunes out of them, we started from the other end of the scale and concentrated on coming up with full songs'.
Chris Slade came in on drums for the departed Simon Wright. Chris was a member of Manfred Mann's Earth Band when they played at the Sydney gig

Malcolm Young attended in 1971. He recalled his audition to *Eonmusic* in 2018:

> I did the audition along with a hundred other, might I say, top players. I won't give you any names, but some of them are household names as far as drummers are concerned. I was the hundredth drummer that they tried out over quite a few months. I didn't think I'd done very well at all. I drove home and I got lost because I was so preoccupied, and it was only an hour from my house. I was berating myself driving home: 'Well, why did you say that? Why did you do that?' and when I got to my house, my wife came up the path and said, 'How did you do?' I said, 'Really badly. I don't think there's much chance of that', and she said, 'They've just called to say you've got the gig!'

Another change was Brian dropping out of writing the lyrics, other than probably a few line changes here and there. The reason given at the time for this was that he was preoccupied with sorting out his divorce from his wife Carol. However, he later told *Rolling Stone* in 2022 that 'I think that was a management decision. It wasn't anything to do with me: 'Listen, Brian, I think the boys are going to write all the lyrics now'. I said: 'It'll give me a little bit of rest not having to worry about coming up with something every now and again'. I never thought of it that much'. Malcolm recalled the writing process to *Guitar World* in July 2008:

> When Angus came up with 'Thunderstruck', I thought, 'Fuck, we've got a great track here'. And that set the standard for that album. Also, during the tour before that (for *Blow Up Your Video*), my drinking had gotten really out of hand. So I decided to take a little breather from the band, and that gave me a bit more time there to mess around with ideas. I started using some keyboards, just sampling the guitar into it for the sake of trying something different. It was interesting, but after that album, I decided I was done with keyboards. Couldn't be bothered any more with that shit!

Chris Slade explained to *Eonmusic* how they laid down the tracks:

> The band, no matter who the drummer is, always play together, all the time, take after take, all day long. That's what they do. We probably played 'Thunderstruck' for days, as with all the other songs on *The Razor's Edge*. Brian sung every song as well, by the way, every time. So, we're in the studio together, all playing together. And that's the way they work. They always have done that and they always will do that.

Chris's statement about Brian always being there to sing as well is interesting because Brian's difficulty on the album is the key of the songs, which often push his voice beyond his range. He could have done with dropped keys and more time to record his vocals.

All in all, this is a very good album with one solid classic in 'Thunderstruck'. If it was reduced to ten tracks, dropping two of the weaker tunes, it would have made for an even better album. But this was the CD age and bands were encouraged to make longer albums. Fraser says, 'I have a favourite on every album I've worked on with them, and many great memories, but I think my favourite album was *Razors Edge* and 'Thunderstruck' my favourite song'.

A great cover would have topped this package off nicely, but it's a poor effort. The CD age never helped anyone's design elements, but what we got was an uninteresting razor cut revealing the album title. The title is reasonable enough, but it's a mystery to me why they didn't call the album 'Thunderstruck'.

One known out-take, which has never been released, was called 'Hard On'.

'Thunderstruck'

During the *Blow Up Your Video* tour, Angus decided to visit his wife's parents in Holland after the Stockholm gig on 26 March 1988. After his visit, he boarded a small plane to take him to the Berlin gig (28 March) and the aircraft was struck by lightning while en route. Fortunately, the plane and passengers got through the incident. Inspired by the incident, Angus started to write 'Thunderstruck'. He recalled to *Apple Music's Essential Music Show* in 2021 that 'It started off as a practice thing on an acoustic guitar I had at home. I had a cassette and I was fiddling around with the guitar and I thought, 'That's interesting', so I put it down'. Angus played it to his brother, who saw the potential. 'Malcolm said, 'that's a little hooky thing, there's something about that'.

Angus took a week away from the recording sessions. He told the *Essential Music Show* what happened when he returned: 'Malcolm came to me and he said, 'Listen and hear what we've done to your song'. I put it on and he had added the big thunder choruses at the beginning and the chant, which we originally only put in the middle section of the song'. Angus was impressed, telling Malcolm: 'You've made it better, you've improved it, you've given it life!' Fraser singles the song out:

One of the best moments of recording that record was during 'Thunderstruck'. We had most of the song recorded and Bruce said to the band that he thought there should be some kind of intro. Angus said that he was working on an idea for it and wanted to try something. He sat on a stool with his guitar, put a lit smoke in his mouth and I rolled the tape. Angus started playing the 'wheedle-a wheedle-a' part. It was only supposed to go in the intro, but he kept playing through the whole song. I wasn't about to stop the tape! He even did the slow-down at the end; it was amazing! When we finally stopped the tape, the long ash on his smoke was still balanced there!

That call-to-arms iconic intro riff is just magnificent, though it could have done with being louder. Listen carefully and you can hear how this was probably developed from Angus's solo in 'Dirty Deeds', which is similar. The riff is so well-known and familiar it's possible to miss what is going on in the engine room. The catchy, thrusting rhythm Malcolm plays dovetails perfectly with Angus and is a wonderful piece of work from him. Focus on it sometime, if you haven't already done so because it's well worth it.

Brian and the backing vocalists come in for the repeated 'thunder' and the first verse. He releases that tension at 1:50 with 'You've been thunderstruck'. That cues the whole band in for the driving rhythm while Angus keeps up the song's main riff. Brian gives one of the most intense, full-on performances of his life for this song. His enthusiasm and passion pour out of every phrase. The cool-down outro, with the riff slowing down, makes for a perfect ending.

On stage, the song took on an extra dimension, with the crowd adding to the opening 'thunder'. It's a truly outstanding live song and one of the very best from the Brian era. Angus singled the song out to *Loudwire* in 2020 as his all-round favourite: 'If it's for a whole song, 'Thunderstruck' is a big one. I like that answer'. It was a big hit, too, as the first single.

'Fire Your Guns'
Angus admitted to the *Auckland Star* in 1990 that the song title is a sexual metaphor, 'but in a little way, you know, nothing too deep, just fire your guns, have a good time'. This is the shortest track on the album, clocking in at under three minutes. The sharp, spasmodic guitars are underpinned by a rock-steady rhythm. It's an AC/DC up-tempo rocker and a good one without being any better than that.

'Moneytalks'
Why the title is one word and not two is a puzzle! It's a highly commercial song with a great groove and a terrific, rolling guitar riff. Brian sticks to his mid-range, which suits him down to the ground. They dial things up for the big sing-along chorus. It's not vintage AC/DC; it's too close to being a pop song on the verses.

It was released as a single in November 1990 and got to number 36 in the UK and 23 in the USA. Australia got the best single release, as they had the at-that-time unreleased 'Down On The Borderline' on the B-side.

'The Razor's Edge'
One of the most interesting songs in the Brian era. The intro sees Angus play an almost Spanish guitar-type part before settling into a droning riff. There is a delicious, dark feel to the song that you rarely hear with AC/DC. That's expanded on in the slightly unnerving backing vocals intoning 'razor's edge'. In truth, they are something of an unnecessary nuisance. Better to have pumped them up loud and recorded 'normally' to give the song more impact.

For some listeners, the song might be *too* dark. It also lacks the big punches of AC/DC's best work, but there's more than enough to compensate. Brian doesn't appear till 1:20. He's on good form in the verses and even more so in the big choruses. It's also one of the best tracks Chris Slade plays on - the man is a rock-solid presence throughout and he nails the song! Angus doesn't let the side down either: his solo kicks in at 2:32 and he takes off and flies. The mix could have been better here; it's a bit cluttered for his solo and they could have done with fading down Chris, in particular.

It's the second-best song on the album – nothing can touch 'Thunderstruck'.

'Mistress For Christmas'

Martin Aston in *Auckland Star* in 1990 asked Angus about the continued accusations of sexism, using this song as an obvious talking point. Angus shrugged it off: 'For us, a song like that is good fun and meant to be taken that way. I've never worried about being called sexist. They'll think that anyhow'. You can argue it's a tongue-in-cheek song, but the obvious and cheap nature of the lyrics is just embarrassing. You can easily imagine the 'what rhymes with Christmas?' conversation when they were constructing the lyrics.

It's Christmas from the off, with sleigh bells and a quietly spoken intro from Brian. It sounds like a big riff is coming due to the build-up on the guitars, but it never quite happens. The chorus is simplistically dreadful, too, a real anti-climax. Angus grabs the song and hammers out some squalling lead guitar to inject some excitement, but he fights a losing battle against that lyrically challenged chorus. This is a real damp squib and certainly no Christmas cracker!

'Rock Your Heart Out'

This one doesn't rise much above being filler. The intro riff is bright enough without being anything special. The verses follow the riff pattern and are reasonably good, but the chorus fails to hit the highs that the title suggests is coming. The bright spots are the brief breakdown moments.

'Are You Ready'

A nice build-up with droning riffs begins proceedings. From there, it's straight into the chorus. The band only do that occasionally, but it always works well. The rhythm track is a solid thump and groove, but I miss Phil Rudd on it. His touch would have suited the rhythm better than Chris Slade. The guitars are great on this; both Malcolm and Angus really make the song rock. The gang-style vocals, whether on their own or interweaving with Brian, hark back to Lange. Indeed, the whole song has those extra 'commercial' touches, so it's no wonder that it was picked as the third single. It was released in March 1991 and reached number 34 in the UK.

'Got You By The Balls'

This is a great song and one of the closest to Phil Rudd-style dynamics on the album. It helps that it goes back to their roots in more ways than most of the album. It's a cracker from the intro, with a fabulous hard riff coming in on one speaker, then joined on the other speaker. The Youngs are doubling the riff as only they can! The chorus is, of course, basically the title, but it works, still riding on the riff that defines the song. With some extra touches, this song would have been even better.

'Shot Of Love'

This is a hidden gem of a song, with the band rocking out and having fun. The intro is all crash, bang, wallop without much point to it, but as soon as the groove comes in after just 14 seconds, we are off and rocking. The power of that groove and the slicing rhythm guitar, plus the strummed chords over the top, is delicious. It has a real Rolling Stones feel to it. It gets even better when Angus starts firing off the lead licks. All this and a great vocal makes it one of the best songs.

'Let's Make It'

One of the worst songs on the album and in the whole back-catalogue. They try to reach for past glories, noticeably so in the chorus, but it just isn't good enough. One to swiftly pass by.

'Goodbye And Good Riddance To Bad Luck'

An unusually verbose title. It starts off promisingly with stinging guitar and Chris punctuating it with Rudd-like aplomb. Sadly, it settles down into a rather dull song, with only the guitars adding much in the way of verve. It needed more dynamics and is an under-achiever of a song.

'If You Dare'

A good closing song. A Beatles-esque start is a nice surprise, but business is soon restored with a corking riff. It has a nice twisting feel to it which surmounts the weak chorus. A nice touch to finish the song and album is Brian's burlesque invitation to 'come outside and play'.

Ballbreaker (1995)

Personnel:
Brian Johnson: lead vocals
Angus Young: lead guitar, backing vocals on 'Hold Me Back'
Malcolm Young: rhythm guitar, backing vocals, lead guitar on 'Can't Stand Still'
Cliff Williams: bass, backing vocals
Phil Rudd: drums
Produced by Rick Rubin and Mike Fraser at Ocean Way, Los Angeles and The Record Plant, Los Angeles, between 1994 and 1995
Release date: 26 September 1995
Label: Albert/East West
Highest chart places: Australia: 1, UK: 6, USA: 4
Running time: 49:47
All songs by Angus and Malcolm Young

After five long years, they were back, and while Chris Slade had done a good job for the band, it's fair to say that Phil Rudd's return to the drum stool was ecstatically received. Malcolm told *Lola Da Musica* in 2001 that 'We always had ambitions of getting Phil back; it was just a matter of time for Phil. He just needed time out. He said he wanted back, and it was just waiting for the moment. So we were just putting drummers in there really till we got him back. He is the real sound with the rest of the guys; it's the real deal, you know?' Malcolm's verdict on the years with Simon Wright and Chris Slade was that 'It still sounded like AC/DC, but it didn't have as much oomph under it'.

Chris Slade had, in fact, been there for the start of the sessions in 1994. He recalled to *Eonmusic*:

I'd been doing demos with the guys in London: Angus, Malcolm and myself. Mal was playing bass and Angus was playing rhythm – no lead guitar, just rhythm guitar, which seems very strange, Malcolm being one of the greatest rhythm guitarists ever. But he played bass in these sessions, and that went on for weeks, and they were writing as they were going along as well.

Next, Chris heard that the band were getting ready to record demos. 'I thought, 'Well, the guys are in the studio; I wouldn't mind playing drums', and I put that to them and they said, 'Yeah, come along', so that's what I did again, for weeks and weeks. It was for the next album (*Ballbreaker*) and I demoed every track for that album'.

Chris's tenure was ended when...

...I got a call from Malcolm saying, 'We're going to try Phil out. Apparently, he's straightened himself up and we're going to try him out', and I went, 'Well, I'm gone then, Malcolm. Thanks very much, but...', and he said, 'No, no, we want you to stay on; we don't even know if he can play drums anymore because it's been a while'. I said, 'And you're going to try him out?!' and he said, 'Yeah, well, we've talked to him', and I said, 'Well, I'm gone, and if he can't play drums, that's your problem now, Malcolm'. He said, 'No, we'll keep paying you', and I said, 'I don't care'. And that was it; I resigned right there and then. After I'd left the band, I went to visit Cliff and Brian to have a pint with them. They were all in the same apartment complex. I said, 'Oh, where's Phil?' This is after he's back in the band, and they said, 'Oh, he's upstairs', and I heard him playing, learning my drum tracks, which is a turn-up for the books because I usually have to learn his tracks! So that was a little bit of satisfaction, actually.

Although Rick Rubin is credited as the main producer, there are stories that most of the heavy lifting was down to Mike Fraser. Fraser's take on the production change from Fairbain to Rubin is that 'every producer has their way of doing it. Bruce was very much involved and tried to keep the session moving along so there wasn't any dead space for boredom to set in. That way, every performance was fresh and exciting. Rick was more of a hands-off guy. He liked to pop in every day or so and comment on progress'.

Rubin talked to *Talk Is Jericho* in 2021 about the 'difficulties' he encountered in making the album:

For straight-up rock, AC/DC is perfection. So, it was another dream-come-true scenario that, I will say, was a difficult process. We got off to a bad start because we went to a studio in New York that didn't sound good, and it was a studio that I always wanted to work in (The Record Plant). We tried all these different things; we ended up upholstering the whole dome. We did a million things trying to make it sound good, (but) nothing worked.

Fraser recalls that 'we tried everything we could think of to get a tight drum sound to no avail. Unfortunately, the studio time was prepaid, and the studio wouldn't give us a refund, so we had to spend six weeks there with not much to show for it. Nothing was kept from Power Station'.

Rubin told *Talk Is Jericho* that he *did* try getting the band to leave Power Station early, but Malcolm was not budging. Rubin recalled him saying: 'We did this with Mutt Lange, we went into every studio in Europe. We're staying here, it's a very good studio'. So then, we stayed for another few weeks and the guy said, 'You know what, let's just go to the studio you like'.' Likely, Malcolm was not leaving until they had got their money's worth from Power Station, and you can see his point if that was so. Fraser recalls that 'we moved the session to Ocean Way, LA and re-recorded everything for a second time. It ended up turning out great, but it was a long, frustrating record. It was mixed at The Record Plant, LA'.

Though things went well at Ocean Way, Rubin felt that the damage was now done. 'Those five or six weeks of trying to make the album in this bad-sounding space took a lot of the spark or just the good vibe out of it, which is a shame. It was the first album that the original drummer (referring to Phil Rudd) came back into the band, which was a big deal for me because I thought he was a key component'. As the sessions overran, Rubin ended up having to split his time between *Ballbreaker* and his work on the Red Hot Chilli Peppers' *One Hot Minute*. This is likely the period when Fraser was 'more involved'.

The band sound more 'authentic' than they have for a while, more like AC/DC with Phil. Brian has some hard moments at times trying to get the notes and power he used to have. He does well, but it's not till *Stiff Upper Lip* that we hear them tackling the issue by dropping the keys to suit his voice. Musically, there is a sense that the tempos are pulled back, and this is pretty much their go-to style from this album on. It works; it's AC/DC, but the higher tempo likes of 'Shake A Leg', 'Brain Shake', etc., are off the radar.

The end result is that this is AC/DC with a purity and intent that had been missing for some time, and all the better for its return. At its best, *Ballbreaker* is a great album with the perfect title. Even the average songs are a cut above what might normally be expected, making it the most consistent album since, at least, *Flick Of The Switch*.

Adding to the sense that AC/DC were back on form was the cover by David McMacken for Marvel Comics, which was the best for a long time. The central strong image of Angus was taken by Robert Ellis back in 1982, but it's the CD booklet with graphic illustrations for every song that sells it.

'Hard As A Rock'
AC/DC back with Phil and opening with a classic. Does it get better than that? The ringing opening riff is sublime, along with Cliff's bass pulse and Phil's cymbals. Malcolm's strummed rhythm part takes it higher, and then when Phil's drums come in, you are in heaven. The Rudder is back! As for Brian, the man is on fire: great vocals and a titanic performance. Just listen to the power he gets in on the verses and the extra strength he injects in the choruses. It's one of his strongest vocals on the album.

Lyrically, it's clear where we are going, but you have to smile at the title's suggestive innuendo, which, by their standards, is almost subtle. Subtle enough that the song was released as the first single from the album. It is the best song here and one that should have stayed in the live set.

'Cover You In Oil'
The tempo drops and the boogie rhythms are back for a guitar shuffle. The song's best aspect is the interplay between Angus and the three-man rhythm machine. When he comes in at the 34-second mark, it pushes the energy levels into the red! The power of the twin rhythm guitars is a marvel.

It wasn't, though, the best choice for track two; I would rather they had kept the pressure up with 'Burnin' Alive', but this is a decent enough song.

It's let down by an uninspiring chorus, which has the feel of a lighter-weight *Back In Black*-era song but without the class. It was released as the third single from the album, backed with 'Love Bomb' and 'Ballbreaker'.

'The Furor'
This one is a dig at the TV evangelists, who seemed to be everywhere at the time. The dictionary meaning is 'a display of public anger or excitement', but Brian's pronunciation of the word sounds mighty close to 'Fuhrer' (a different meaning altogether), as evidenced by the chorus line of 'I'm your furor'.

It opens with a killer twin guitar intro along with Phil's hi-hat. Once Cliff's bass comes in, we are off and away. The blend of the guitars is one of the best aspects. Malcolm keeping it simple with the clean low notes, while the busy higher notes, mixed slightly lower, are by Angus. It shows how great these two work together. It harks back to 'Send For The Man' in the dark-toned verses.

Brian goes for the top of his range and sounds uncomfortable. It's a good example of how a song could have worked better if they had dropped the key for him. In spite of that, it's a good enough song and Angus's solo hits the spot.

'Boogie Man'
Time for some blues. The title says it all, with Cliff and Phil locking in for a slow groove. The band always enjoy taking it down like this and there's really nothing more to it (save the powerful outro) other than the slow-rolling rhythms. They find a different gear for the chorus, but it's not a huge step up, more like a stronger affirmation of the verses! Phil's cymbal accents are great, especially under Angus's wailing solo. It's a real stunner, too, and you can imagine the smiles from the band when he came up with that one. He gets in another one all the way to the outro for good measure.

'The Honey Roll'
The riff has one of those turnaround licks at the end that adds a little more interest, in the same way that the riff to 'Back In Black' also has it. The brothers double the riff and the subsequent basic strutting riff. They work between the two riffs throughout the song, which is interesting, but other than that, there's not much else here of note. It's the weakest track on the album and needed something else to raise the standard.

'Burnin' Alive'
The real events that inspired the lyrics are the 1993 Waco massacre in the USA and the awful manner of the cult followers' deaths. It's rare for AC/DC to write about anything outside of sex and rock 'n' roll, but there you have it. Subject matter aside, it's the music that sells this one.

The low pulse intro (reminiscent of 'Live Wire') sets things up beautifully for the riff. What an exciting earworm of a riff it is, too; melodic and musical yet as hard as steel. It sits in with the monstrous groove, which has a great drum part from Phil. He shows exactly what they had been missing here. Angus goes for a bluesy solo, which is the perfect counterpoint to the melody and underlines the drama in the lyrics.

This is one of the best songs on the album. Brian is at his croakiest on it, but somehow, that doesn't matter too much. He gives it 100%, as he always does.

'Hail Caesar'
Angus's interest in gladiators also probably inspired this one. The intro is interesting, with the Youngs strumming some menacing chords. They keep the feel going for the verses, featuring a great twisting riff which interplays with Brian. The chorus, by contrast, is a gang-style shout-out, perfect for a live setting. If anything, they don't make that chorus as big as it should be; the backing vocals needed to be boosted a lot more and the backing track given more power.

The solo is excellent and leads directly into the bridge (2:56), which is the best part of the song. They dial it right down for Brian and he delivers this astonishing vocal that is eerily close to Bon Scott in his phrasing and nuances. The backing here is a masterclass in keeping things tight and interesting. From there to the outro, the band find an extra gear and the song explodes into life. It was released as the second single from the album.

'Love Bomb'
One of the weaker tracks. It sounds like they had a desirable title without any great ideas to go with it. It might be the most repeated title in an AC/DC song! Another contender would be 'Back In Black', but the quality of that song is so immense that you don't register it as a negative. Here, the title stands out because the backing track is average at best. Brian's voice has a hard time, which doesn't help matters. The riff over the verses steers close to The Kinks' 'You Really Got Me', which is no bad thing but not enough to save this mediocre track.

'Caught With Your Pants Down'
It's got a lighter feel of 'Rosie' throughout much of the song. Overall, this is one of the best workouts between the brothers on the album. It really is their show once they get into the swing at the 53-second mark. While the song is otherwise pretty limited, the raw guitars plus the drive of the rhythm section keep you listening. It's not great, but it's better than average.

'Whiskey On The Rocks'
This is another of the better tracks, beginning with a slow burner intro featuring ringing guitar that nods to 'Hard As Rock'. The chorus showcases

Angus's ringing high notes over the dirty rhythm with that deep, ingrained, satisfying AC/DC feel to it. They don't push the chorus as much as they could have done, but it works. The title is a gift to Brian, who gets a lot of mileage out of singing it. It's not quite a top-drawer song, but it is very good. Ideally, this would have been a baseline minimum standard of quality for the album. If everything was, at least, as good as this, the album would have been right up just behind *Back In Black*.

'Ballbreaker'
This is easily one of the best on the album and a seriously great AC/DC song. The catchy intro lick is clever. Once round on one guitar, the lick is then doubled and more powerful the second time around, with Phil crashing in on the end of each phrase. It's a great setup for the riff that then kicks in. And what a riff it is, a coruscating thing of wonder underpinned by the Cliff/Phil throbbing groove and a powerhouse vocal from Brian. The precision and deliberation of the riff hit like a ball-breaker. Job done there! When the solo comes in (1:58), it gets a bit soupy in the mix – the sharp clarity has gone. The riff is still there but dropped back into the rhythm. You can hear the change again at 2:53 when they revert to the verses – the sound is much cleaner again. The outro is another solo section, with Brian interjecting the title for good measure. What a big beast to finish the album off!

Ballbreaker Rehearsals
These emerged in fan circles and are easy to find on YouTube. It's the band jamming and trying out ideas and you can tell they are having a lot of fun. AC/DC are by no means a sterile band, but the playfulness you hear on these songs would have been quite welcome if it had crept into their albums more, as, say, it did with 'Gone Shootin''. The titles of the tracks are likely fan creations based on the official titles when possible.

'Boogie Man' is rooted in the blues standard 'I'm A Man' ('Mannish Boy'). You can hear how they jumped off from this to the version on the album, but this is a more deeply authentic take on the blues than the released song. It's a delight. 'Jailhouse Rock Jam' may lyrically borrow from the Elvis song, but the backing track is pure 'Peter Gunn'. You can hear the origin of the riff to 'Caught With Your Pants Down' making a brief appearance here, too. 'Blues Jam' is exactly that, a 12-bar blues that keeps repeating. Right at the end is a tantalising snatch of the riff from 'Hail Caesar'.

'Burnin' Alive' is taken at a slower, more deliberate tempo than the released version as the band feel through the changes. Phil's snare is right up front and sounds great! The sparser, raw feel of this take is engaging.

'Caesar Salad' (great title) starts as another 12-bar blues. Once past that, they try out parts of 'Hail Caesar'. Brian runs through the bridge breakdown section softly to himself while waiting for the Youngs to come back in with the riff. At 2:48, you get the Bo Diddley riff from 'Not Fade Away', which

Brian can't resist singing along to. At the end, Angus strums the intro to 'Hard As A Rock'.

'Louisiana Swamp Stomp' features Angus playing slide guitar. The main body of this instrumental is a blues jam and it's his guitar that stands out. It's not overly interesting, but then we were never supposed to hear it in the first place!

'She's My Babe' is the final song and where it all gets very interesting. The spritely backing track is based on Elmore James's 'Madison Blues' (as popularised by Fleetwood Mac and George Thorogood). Brian has a full set of lyrics (maybe ad-libbed, but they work) and this sounds like it was close to being a fully-fledged song, as it is so worked up and ready. It would have made a great bonus track or B-side and is well worth checking out.

Stiff Upper Lip (2000)

Personnel:
Brian Johnson: lead vocals
Angus Young: lead guitar, backing vocals
Malcolm Young: rhythm guitar, backing vocals, guitar solo on 'Can't Stand Still'
Cliff Williams: bass, backing vocals
Phil Rudd: drums
Produced by George Young at The Warehouse, Vancouver, between September and November 1999
Release date: 28 February 2000
Label: East West
Highest chart places: Australia: 3, UK: 12, USA: 7
Running time: 46:57
All songs by Angus and Malcolm Young

The Youngs started writing new material soon after the end of the *Ballbreaker* tour. While the *Bonfire* box set in 1997 was a welcome distraction, fans were eagerly awaiting a new album. That was stymied by Malcolm revealing they had abandoned the songs they were working on. So, it was back to square one. Angus and Malcolm started work on new demos in March 1998 and it took 18 months to come up with enough material for the album. Mike Fraser was back again, but, as he recounts, there was a change in producer:

The band were originally going to get Bruce Fairbairn to produce again, but unfortunately, he passed away (on 17 May 1999). George (Young) was retired by then, but Mal and Ang managed to recruit him for one more record. It was great working with George; he was a fantastic guy. He would kind of let Mal and Ang do their thing and would chime in when a decision needed to be made. It was great to watch the dynamics between the three brothers. I could imagine them making the early records.

Brian put it like this to *Guitar World* in 2000: 'With the three brothers working together again, it's just the climax of many years of doing the right thing with music'.

They entered The Warehouse in September 1999 with 18 songs and spent nearly three months working the best 13 up. One ('Cyberspace') was kept for a bonus track/B-side. Missing from the production team was Harry Vanda, but Brian was quick to see that there were positives to that, as he outlined to *Guitar World* in 2000:

Not detracting from Harry, but it was kinda streamlined this time. You had no one to answer to or discuss things with except Malcolm or Angus. We were working pretty hard this time, from about 11 in the morning until one the next morning sometimes. Saturdays as well. It was good, though. George always had a game plan. I hate it when you're hanging around waiting for the next decision. George always had it all worked out.

Cliff told VH1's *Behind The Music* in 2000 that it was 'a killer album. It was a very easy-to-record album in as much as Malcolm and Angus had everything ready to go, so we basically just had to come along and perform as best we could'.

Angus detailed their approach to recording the basic tracks to *Guitar World* in 2000. 'We all get in there. That's what makes rock and roll. You lose that when you start separating everything up. You can separate things technically by isolating your amps, but when we're in there recording, we all like to be together so we can all communicate easily'. As for guitar overdubs, he explained that 'If Mal has a little added rhythm part, or if I have a lick here or there, that'll make it different. Or we might just use the basic track. Whatever gives it the best atmosphere'. Fraser confirms that 'most of the time with recording AC/DC, it's about spending the time to get great sounds on all the instruments and being ready to record right away once they plug in their guitars. This record was no exception. They go out into the recording room and rock!'

It was Angus who came up with the *very* AC/DC title, as he told *Guitar World* in 2000: 'I was thinking that one of the earliest images of rock 'n' roll that I'd ever seen was Elvis Presley, who always had that big old lip sticking straight up in the air, that sneer, you know? And that's something that's carried straight through rock 'n' roll. Hendrix, Jagger, they all had that thing with the lip'. The cover shot of Angus as a statue, set against a New York skyscraper backdrop, is strong and effective if being rather reminiscent of *Ballbreaker* in style.

What runs through the album is a strong vein of the blues and rock 'n' roll that they had touched on again with *Ballbreaker*. Overall, it's an excellent solid album. There's a stone-cold classic in the title track, the excellent 'Hold Me Back' and several other very good songs. Even the lesser tracks have something to warrant repeated listens. At least four other tracks were recorded: 'The Cock Crows', 'Let It Go', 'Rave On' and 'Whistle Blower'. None have yet emerged officially or otherwise.

'Stiff Upper Lip'

This is the strongest song on the album, as you might expect, with it being the opening track. Fraser loves it as well: 'One of my faves, too. It's a great riff and toe-tapper. It was a fun song to do'. That fun comes across in every note. It's pure class right from the intro, with the sinuous riff grabbing your attention, along with Phil's cymbals and Brian's scene-setting, low-register vocal.

That 24-second bluesy intro is shattered by the steamroller rhythm track, with that riff still going but doubled by the brothers. Brian is on top form here, as is Phil, whose cymbal splashes keep it all moving forward. Angus's solo is a blues walkabout that touches on Billy Gibbons' best work with ZZ Top. It's one of those that complements the melody rather than being totally out there and self-indulgent. But the licks he adds here and there are amazing, especially the slides he plays from 2:36, where Brian excitedly cries, 'and I shoot, shoot, shoot from the hip'. From there, it's a euphoric rush to the end. How they sound this potent after all these years is a thing of wonder. It was the first single from the album and deserved to do a lot better than it did.

'Meltdown'

The change of tempo and feel is a letdown after 'Stiff Upper Lip'. It needed something up there as potent as the title track for the perfect one-two opening. It's more than a bit repetitive and is one of the weaker songs on the album. There's not much lift in the chorus and even Angus can't pick things up with his solo. The droning outro with a slowing drum beat is unexpected and is the best part of the song. Overall, this one could have been much better.

'House Of Jazz'

The lyrics were inspired by a place that the Youngs had rented in California for rehearsals. It would have made a better track two than 'Meltdown', which it has some base similarities to as a laid-back groove song. The big difference is the nagging, insistent guitar riff and the strong chorus.

In spite of the title, there's a distinct lack of jazz to this one. The riff is a real earworm, a gem that keeps coming at you. Phil's crash cymbals punctuate the riff to great effect and you have to like the way he ups the tempo for the chorus. Brian's vocal mirrors the riff, both adopting a similar skipping momentum. It all makes for a very good song.

'Hold Me Back'

This is a supremely catchy song. Everything gels together and works brilliantly. The intro, with Cliff and Phil slightly behind the beat, is pure gold. Then Malcolm's rhythm riff kicks in, Angus doubles it and they're off. Phil is a monster here, slamming home the beat, aided by emphatic cymbal crashes. The movement in the rhythm is terrific; you can feel it so deep inside that it's hard not to move along with it! This is topped off in the chorus with a melody line from Angus that is another 'Shoot To Thrill'-like thing of wonder. I love how they turn up the volume for the big ending. For me, this is one of the best on the album and one of the best full-stop from the Brian era.

'Safe In New York City'

'I suppose that song is a little tongue-in-cheek', said Angus to *Guitar World* in 2000. 'Last time I was in New York, that's all people were talking about, how safe it was, how it was gonna be such a great place to live. For me, New York has always been a city of unpredictability. You can never guess what's going to happen next'. Brian, to the same magazine, also, pointed out that 'the lads had a bit of fun with that song 'cause, in the end, they stuck in that little line, 'I'd feel safe in a cage in New York City'. Just in case people start fuckin' believing it!'.

This busy, bustling song has a high-octane, nervy riff that keeps things interesting. Brian doesn't have much to work with here, but he manages to hold your attention. The contrast between the riff and the mantra-like chorus (of the title) is intriguing. However, the lyrics let it down and the chorus doesn't hit the high spots. It was released as a single, giving fans the chance to pick up 'Cyberspace' on the B-side.

'Can't Stand Still'

They play it basic and simple, and Brian, for one, was overjoyed. 'Aye, that's one of my favourites. I don't think I've heard anything like that played that well before. It just gets me all goosebumpy every time I hear the flippin' thing', he told *Guitar World* in 2000.

The melodic lead run is the main interest, but it distracts from Brian because it's such a busy line. Malcolm's rare lead guitar solo is a treat and it's a shame we didn't get more from him. They save the best till the outro, with an almost burlesque ending and a surprise for Brian: 'Every time we'd go in and cut a track, Brian was singing along with us for the vibe', Angus told *Guitar World*. 'And on that one, he was really hammering it out. We were getting off on watching him do it. Everyone was having a little fun with it. So, when it came to the ending, everybody sort of downed tools and gave him a little ripple'. To which Brian responds in the song with an amused, 'Thank you lads'.

'Can't Stop Rock 'N' Roll'

Angus was aware of the view being espoused around this time that rock 'n' roll was dead. 'That song is our little statement on that', he told *Guitar World* in 2000. He continued:

Our whole career has been playing rock 'n' roll. And I'm sure you still get a lot of people tuning in to bands like us and The Stones. And younger bands will be plugging into it and taking it into the next realm. There's always going to be another generation that will take it and give it to a new, younger audience. So, I think it will just keep going on.

That combative view is there in the droning intro riff. The verses are from the 'Back In Black' ballpark, musically, but Brian isn't as convincing; you can hear that the key is too high for him. There's a rather pedestrian tempo that holds things back. They try to liven it up, such as when Angus's solo lifts off at 2:33, and the outro has some vibrancy. It should have been a lot better.

'Satellite Blues'

A crunching opening riff, cymbals and a distant jubilant 'yay' open this unheralded gem. It's not till the first chorus that a second rhythm guitar is added. It makes the chorus just explode with power, and from there, the song rolls along with a killer snap to it. Cliff even gets in some fat, funky bass notes for colour (the first appears at 1:12). The waves of choruses all the way to the outro, with Angus soloing over the top, make for a terrific ending. Some territories got this as the third single from the album.

'Damned'

The intro's slow, deliberate riff, with just Phil accompanying, is highly effective. Then in comes Brian for his first verse. The space in the sound here, with just the three of them, allows the song to breathe and really heightens the impact. It's quite a jolt when the second rhythm guitar comes in at the 33-second mark. Cliff is delayed further still till 59 seconds. The full band sound proves as impressive as the intro. Now, here's the smart bit – they repeat the formula. They back off from the full band back down to a minimal sound before the full band comes back in again! It's a good ploy, and this, plus scorching mid-song and outro solos from Angus, mark this song out as an overlooked gem.

'Come And Get It'

A melodic, playful guitar sound is a good counterpoint to the simple rhythm. They manage to up things in the catchy chorus, which features amusingly deadpan backing vocals. There's not much else of note here. It's not quite a filler track, but it isn't far off.

'All Screwed Up'

A sublime, buzzing, doubled intro riff from the Youngs is the big draw. But credit must also go to Phil, who is excellent, especially with the thwacking beat he gets in at the end of each riff. It makes for a catchy tune, which sadly loses some impetus with the weak chorus. It speeds up in the long outro, which adds extra verve and interest. But the best thing is that rhythm track, which I could listen to on repeat. It's not a great song other than that, but it's worth its place on the album.

'Give It Up'

The riff reminds me of 'If You Want Blood'. Whatever, this one has quite a Bon-era sound to it. It's got that toughness in the verses and the full-on melodic but still heavy chorus they do so well. What it isn't is a closing track, but this is something AC/DC have often had trouble with – that closing big banger. It's still up there with the better songs on the album.

Additional Track

'Cyberspace'

This pacey rocker would have upped the overall tempo of the album if it had been included. It has a great energy level, but it's let down by a very weak chorus that does little to grab you. This was released on the 'Safe In New York City' single and also appeared on tour editions of *Stiff Upper Lip*.

Black Ice (2008)

Personnel:
Brian Johnson: lead vocals
Angus Young: lead guitar, slide guitar on 'Stormy May Die'
Malcolm Young: rhythm guitar, backing vocals
Cliff Williams: bass, backing vocals
Phil Rudd: drums
Produced by Brendan O'Brien at The Warehouse, Vancouver, between 3 March
and 25 April 2008
Release date: 20 October 2008
Label: East West
Highest chart places: Australia: 1, UK: 1, USA: 1
Running time: 55:38
All songs by Angus and Malcolm Young

It had been a little over eight years since AC/DC recorded *Stiff Upper Lip*.
There had been a now-customary time off between albums, but there were
additional delays. The band left their long-time home of Atlantic Records in
2002 and signed with Sony Music imprint Epic Records. *Billboard* reported
in December that the multi-album deal would include refurbished reissues of
their old albums. *Billboard* also noted that 'It is understood that AC/DC's next
studio album, due sometime next year, will complete the group's contractual
obligation to Elektra'. As that release never happened, clearly, some sort of
extra deal must have been struck. A further delay was caused by changes
within Sony itself, which saw the band shift from Epic to Columbia.

The biggest delay was caused by a serious accident in 2005 involving Cliff
Williams. It left him unable to play bass for 18 months. He explained what
happened to *Bass Player* in 2021:

I took a fall and put my hand out to break my fall right onto some broken
glass. It cut the nerves and tendons in my left hand. I had two surgeries
for that and lots of rehab. The guys were awesome; they said, 'Go and get
yourself well and we'll pick it up from there'. Now I can only play with two
fingers, the two on the outsides. The two middle fingers I just keep out of
the mix. I've learned how to do that. I've got flexibility straight up and down,
so I can make a fist, but when I try and bend those fingers individually, they
don't bend. The surgeon was brilliant, but a couple of the tendons let loose,
and I felt them when they did, so it was bad. But you stick with it and you
get around it. Thank God there's only four strings on the damn thing. I never
looked at it as 'I'm never gonna play again'; I just took the attitude that I've
just gotta get over this and get it done.

The positive news was that the Youngs managed to stockpile plenty of
material. They had around 60 to 70 ideas and the plan was to record 18 songs

and pick the best 11. Fraser says, 'We just rocked away until the dust settled at the end of the recordings and then saw what we had'. In the end, they opted for 15 songs, which made for their longest album yet. The remaining three songs, plus other material, would be looked at again for *Rock Or Bust*.

Brendan O'Brien produced the album and he encouraged the band to come up with the big melodies that marked out their most widely popular songs, such as 'You Shook Me All Night Long'. He also suggested the band tune down to make things easier for Brian, who consequently sounded better than he had in a long time. Fraser found O'Brien to be...

...cool to work with. He was a little more hands-on than the previous producers. He's a great guitar player in his own right, so sometimes, to explain his thoughts, he would pick up a guitar to show what he meant. He didn't write riffs or anything, but he could explain a tempo thing or arrangement thing easier by playing it rather than explaining it.

Sonically, this is a brighter, bigger-sounding album than the previous two, which is evident right from the opening notes. If *Black Ice* had been made up of the best eight or ten songs, it would have been an even stronger album, arguably their best since *Back In Black*. The album title was originally *Runaway Train*, with the cover art based on the photograph of the Gare-Montparnasse (in Paris) rail derailment on 22 October 1895. The band soon found that Mr. Big had used the same image for their 1991 album *Lean Into It* – back to the drawing board. As a title, *Black Ice* doesn't cut it and neither does the forgettable cover.

Angus later commented to *Rolling Stone* in November 2014 that symptoms of Malcolm's dementia 'first started appearing while we were making *Black Ice*'. Sadly, it would be the last album and supporting tour for Malcolm Young.

'Rock 'N' Roll Train'
The original idea was from Angus, who told *Guitar World* in February 2009:

Malcolm picked that out of a whole batch of ideas. He said, 'That one's a really good track, a bit different'. I didn't see it. I'm going, 'Are you sure?' But as soon as Malcolm heard it, he had the idea for that vocal melody in the chorus ('Train right on the track'). Malcolm's always good at that. He can show me how to spread an idea out and get the best out of it.

It is the album's best track, as usual, being the opening banger. Fraser heartily concurs:

Again, this showcased another classic AC/DC riff. Originally, the working title was 'Runaway Train', but that title was already taken. We ended up having to redo the chorus vocals and change the words. At first, I didn't like the change, but it grew on me, and now I can't imagine it being anything but 'Rock 'n' Roll Train'.

In fact, they only change the first line of each chorus, as Brian sings 'rock 'n' roll' instead of 'runaway'. Every other line keeps to 'runaway train'. It's a stunner of an opening riff; you know who it is straight away from that alone. And then the instant joy of Phil's drums cueing in the rest of the band. It's such a catchy, solid intro, with Malcolm's lower rhythm guitar and Angus's higher rhythm weaving around him. The first verse instantly sounds clear and controlled because Brian is well within his register and all the better for it. The riff is still present and correct for the first verse, but the second ('Give it all, give it, give it what you got') sees a longer riff come in that is the perfect counterpoint to the main riff, adding a different feel to the song. They don't fail on the chorus either, which is pure stadium sing-along heaven! You can almost feel Angus waiting for his solos. He finally kicks in at 2:26 with a flurry of notes, but he gets out again after just 17 seconds! However, as they head into the outro, he pops up everywhere with melodic fills and blasts of guitar. It's a great ending to an AC/DC classic. It was released as a single backed with 'War Machine'.

'Skies On Fire'
Phil's opening groove is glorious, and once the big guitars and bass come in, we are talking prime AC/DC. The constant switch from a jangly guitar tone (choruses) to a deeper, more primal sound (verses) is a neat touch. The chorus is big and melodic, with the harmony vocals really adding to the overall effect. It's another one to sing along to!

'Big Jack'
Lyrically, this is pure nonsense, with a chorus that doesn't hit the mark and that squirm-inducing line (from Brian) of 'Santa ain't the only one who's got a full sack'. The best thing about it is the superb engine room of Malcolm, Cliff and Phil. Somehow, it made the live setlist, where it was exposed even more as a makeweight alongside the more illustrious material. Incredibly, it was picked out as the second single.

'Anything Goes'
This is outside the box, a different flavour for the band, with a more classic rock approach than usual. It's bright and almost (whisper it) a pop song. It only just made the cut, being the last song recorded. Angus recalled to Alan Di Perna for *Guitar World* in February 2009 that 'Malcolm had that one when he came to Vancouver'. He said, 'I'll just play it and see what you think'. And everyone liked it. On his demo, he had the drone going. It was a case of capturing the feel of it and adding a little bit of colour here and there'. That opening drone is set against the poppier melody played by Angus. This could

be by one of many bands, and it's mostly down to Phil and the solos and fills from Angus that give it the AC/DC identity. It's a good song that's worth its place on the album. It was also the third single.

'War Machine'
There's a real hint of menace in Malcolm's rhythm playing and Cliff's prominent bass that gives the backing track that extra punch. The verses are fine, but the chorus misses its mark. A good song that could have been improved.

The idea for the lyrics came from a TV programme. Angus told *Guitar World* in February 2009:

> I was watching a thing about Hannibal, who went over the Alps with the elephants to defeat the Romans. When Rome was in power, there was another empire: the Carthaginian Empire. But this senator guy in Rome said, 'They got the best wine, the best oil, the best of everything in Carthage'. He was basically whipping up the populace: 'We're gonna get you in a war'. The soldiers were paid in wheat, and they were promised they'd get bigger handouts of wheat. Of course, when they came back, they got shat on after doing the dirty work. I thought, 'Well, nothing's changed!'

'Smash 'N' Grab'
This is a decent track despite a very trebly sound. They give the gang vocal chorus full effort and it's the best part of the song. The guitar parts are well blended with the choppy rhythm riff and complementary top-line notes. At times, it sounds like there's a guitar synth in the mix, with some brassy-sounding interjections. It's worth its place on the album.

'Spoilin' For A Fight'
The Youngs stockpiled some classic riffs in their time away. Here's another beauty: a catchy thrusting earworm of a riff that opens and powers the song. Once they hit the throbbing groove, with the riff still there, we are off into AC/DC heaven.

There are the glorious parts where the band really let rip, such as the section which kicks in hard from 2:10, with Angus's stinging solo over the rhythm track. This is a decent track which could have been even better with a stronger chorus.

'Wheels'
Brian is at the top end of his register here on this vibrant, lively song. The chorus is the biggest stretch for him on the album, and indeed, the backing vocalists! It's no wonder this was never in the live set. The only thing that's lacking here is the chorus. As the band always use the title as the basis for the chorus, it leaves things wanting, as there is little to say!

'Decibel'

A welcome detour back into a blues shuffle gives the album some rootsy authenticity. It's always a pleasure to hear the band in this idiom. It's a great little song, too; you can hear the band thriving on playing it. The lead licks are quite distinct from the shuffle and stand out. When it comes to the solo, Angus fittingly dips into the blues. The chorus isn't the best, but overall, there's enough here to keep me coming back to the song.

'Stormy May Day'

Angus opens the song with a flurry of notes like he is trying to find a riff. After a brief pause, he then lets rip with a wicked slide guitar part. The next nice surprise is Phil's floor tom kicking in before they launch into the groove. With the slide still there, it makes for a deliciously different slant on things. It stays in the same zone for most of the song; you expect it to rise up in power, but it doesn't. Instead, they back off almost completely at 2:39, dropping down to an up-and-personal Brian over a softer backing track, which fades out. The calm after the storm.

The slide guitar part was pushed for by O'Brien. Angus recalled to *Guitar World* in February 2009:

> On the demo I'd done for that song, I got an acoustic guitar, put it on my lap and used a cigarette lighter for a slide. I put it in the background, but Brendan heard that and kept reminding me, 'There's a slide on there'. So, I had to go out there and give it a try. I had one slide from years back that I picked up. It was a really cool bit of Plexiglas, or something, that you wear on the pinkie. My fingers are very small and it fits just right. But when I went to do the track, I couldn't remember where I'd put it. I said, 'Oh well, I'll probably find it one day'. But they went out and found some things that were pretty close, and I used one of those for the track.

'She Likes Rock 'N' Roll'

The opening riff harks back to 'Rock 'N' Roll Train', but you can't knock that. What they do so brilliantly here is to keep it simple: a cutting rhythm and the accents from Angus. Brian manages to get more out of the lyrics than would seem possible. The chorus is simple and dumb, but you just can't knock it for pure irresistibility and there's a great lift and push on it that smashes it home. A real earworm of a song – sometimes, basic works best.

'Money Made'

'You come to this side of the world (America) and everything is money these days', Angus told Alan Di Perna at *Guitar World* in February 2009:

> The focus seems to be, 'How do we get money out of this? Do we keep that school? Is there a profit in it? Do we really need that new hospital? Can

you not die quicker? Do we really have to spend money on that medicine? Sometimes you think, Can we all take one deep breath? The basics have got to be in place. Thirty years ago, a fuckin' school never made money. Filling in a road or putting up a traffic light didn't make money. Hospitals were there to keep people well, not make money.

A snaking arpeggio riff opens this intriguing lyrical diversion for the band. They get the 9 to 5 drudgery across in the tempo and feel. For some extra panache, they flirt close to the 'Back In Black' riff in the verses, which typically makes for great dynamics. You have to love the bridge (2:25), which sees the instrumentation drop down to Malcolm and Phil before Angus comes back in doubling the riff, followed by the return of Cliff and Brian. The song is quite busy, which perhaps explains why there is no guitar solo from Angus. Overall, it's a good song, with that 'borrowed' riff sealing the deal. It was the fourth single from the album.

'Rock 'N' Roll Dream'
A different approach for this one. The soft chorus guitar licks with Angus and Malcolm playing off each other builds the atmosphere up. Brian mirrors the tone, giving a vintage, heartfelt performance. When the song explodes into life, it maintains a reflective quality. The guitar parts are stunning, with Malcolm's rhythm combining beautifully with Angus. I love the pulsing rhythm against the melodic licks and then there's the more urgent overdubbed fills from Angus. This is an excellent song that is a bit lost in this extended running order. On a traditional eight-track album, this would pop out even more.

'Rocking All The Way'
Another one from the 'She Likes Rock 'N' Roll' box. There's a real ZZ Top feel to it in the verses, which set things up for a chorus where they hit a peak. Angus tears off some great solos as well. This is AC/DC keeping things simple and direct and still delivering as only they can. How they can conjure up such joy out of relatively slight material is a rare talent, but they do it. Sometimes simple is best!

'Black Ice'
The title at least came from Brian, but the song lacks the danger inherent in the title. It just isn't as good as the band clearly thought it was; they inexplicably chose it for the live set. The riff is a little over-busy and the chorus doesn't do much to lift the song. It feels like they're trying too hard, but there isn't the substance there. A disappointing end to a strong album.

Conclusion
The ensuing live tour was an enormous success, but Malcolm's issues with dementia had reached a point where it was a huge effort for him to complete

the gigs. A tribute to the man that he got through the schedule at all. I heard first-hand from a security member at the Wembley Arena gigs that the band had a spare guitarist present 'just in case Malcolm couldn't play'. This seems feasible and it would be easy to imagine Stevie Young accompanying them on tour.

Angus told the *Sunday Post* in 2021. About how Malcolm never once lost his never-say-die spirit: 'When he was sick, he had a lot of help on the *Black Ice* tour. He was on medicines. He was even putting down ideas. Whenever I was with him, he'd be saying: 'We keep going as long as I can do it'. Even when he was in hospital for operations, he was the same. He'd be going: 'I want to be with you'.

Rock Or Bust (2014)

Personnel:
Brian Johnson: lead vocals
Angus Young: lead guitar
Stevie Young: rhythm guitar, backing vocals
Cliff Williams: bass, backing vocals
Phil Rudd: drums
Produced by Brendan O'Brien at The Warehouse, Vancouver, between 3 May and 12 July 2014
Release date: 28 November 2014
Label: Columbia
Highest chart places: Australia: 1, UK: 3, USA: 3
Running time: 34:55
All songs by Angus and Malcolm Young

Angus pointed out to *ABC News* in 2014 that 'each album we've ever done was newer stuff and older stuff. I had to go through a lot myself and put ideas together, but Mal kept writing right up till he could do it no more'. The band sensitively announced in April 2014 that Malcolm was 'taking a break' from the band due to ill health. However, Brian told *Rolling Stone* in 2014 that they still intended to go into the studio to make a new album. 'We're going to pick up some guitars, have a plonk and see if anybody has got any tunes or ideas', he said. 'If anything happens, we'll record it'.

There was no doubt that the absence of their driving force was difficult. Brian said to *Rolling Stone* in November 2014:

It was a strange feeling because your workmate you've worked with, for me, for the last 35 years, wasn't there anymore. For Angus, it was more (than that) because it was his brother. But Stevie came in and he's a part of the Young family. He has the same personality as well.

Angus added in the same interview that his nephew was 'like a clone. He grew up that way, playing that hard rhythm style'. Stevie Young was, of course, the obvious choice to step back into the band, having covered for Malcolm before.

Mike Fraser was back and feels the title of the album sums it all up: '*Rock Or Bust* was, I guess, how we all felt about doing a record without Malcolm. He was such an integral part of the whole machine and to carry on without him was a leap of faith. It was gonna rock, or we'd go bust trying. My personal thoughts anyway, I can't speak for the band'.

Brendan O'Brien returned to produce and took on a key role in the final song selection. Angus revealed to *Rolling Stone* in November 2014 that O'Brien had the band 'in and out (of the studio) in four weeks'. He said, 'I'm the big AC/DC fan', so he picked what he thought that fan would want to hear!'

Malcolm's dementia was finally confirmed in September 2014 in an announcement that also confirmed he would be retiring. Little else was said, understandably so, but Angus stated to Rolling Stone in November 2014 that 'He is happy. He's getting a lot of care. His family is with him all the time and they're strong'.

While still coming to terms with Malcolm's situation, the band could have done without the added complication of Phil's arrest. That came on 6 November on charges of drug possession and hiring a hitman for a contract murder! Although the latter charge was dropped, it still left him accused of the possession charge and making death threats.

Angus and Cliff faced a media who were just as keen to know about Phil's story as they were about *Rock Or Bust*. The duo told *Rolling Stone* in November 2014 that they had had their own issues with Phil going back to the recording sessions. 'It was tough to get him there in the first place', said Cliff. Fraser adds that:

I believe there were some immigration issues that needed to be sorted out with Phil. To be honest, I'm not too privy to the behind-the-scenes workings of the band unless it's in the studio. We were all hoping Phil's situation could work out. There was probably a plan B being worked on, but I wasn't aware of what that would be.

Phil made it for the album, but he missed the roll call for the promo photo shoots and the video recording for 'Play Ball' in October. 'It put us in a difficult situation', said Angus. 'I don't know the exact situation. We don't monitor each other in our downtime. I can only say, from our perspective, that the guy needs to sort himself out'. One wonders what Malcolm's take would have been on the matter! Whatever happened with Phil, Angus told *Rolling Stone* that the band had 'decided to move forward, whether Phil wants to be part of it or not'.

The front cover is computer generated and uninteresting, but the packaging is saved by the simple, poignant photograph of Malcolm's and Angus's guitars, with the slogan 'In rock we trust'.

Rock Or Bust is, at its base level, a very good AC/DC album, and parts of it are excellent. The band are on fire and Brian leads from the front with a big performance. The opening one-two punch of 'Rock Or Bust' and 'Play Ball', for instance, is the best they had come up with in quite a while. The album would obviously have been more special if Malcolm had been featured to some degree. Fraser explains that:

It never came up that we'd use a Malcolm track. These guys play live in the studio and never play to a click or backing tracks. Besides, there were no parts from Mal that could ever have been used. Any demos that existed would be stereo files on DAT or cassette and impossible to separate a single guitar from.

There is a strong sense of this being a bits-and-pieces recording; it sounds like curated leftovers (albeit very good ones). The title, though, is an apt summary of where they were at: 'That go-for-broke attitude which we've always had', Angus reflected to *Rolling Stone* in November 2014.

'Rock Or Bust'
It instantly says AC/DC are back, a triumphant blast of a song. The DNA shows through, with a firm nod to 'Back In Black' in the primary riff and 'Nervous Shakedown' in the secondary riff. Everything is there in place: Cliff's pulse, Phil's trademark just off-the-beat drums and Stevie Young doing his uncle Malcolm proud on rhythm guitar. At the forefront, Angus smashes the lead licks. I love the ecstatic solo he plays in the chorus. Brian is probably the man of the match here, leading from the front with the powerhouse vocal they needed, and boy, does he deliver! Angus holds back from his solo until 1:57, but once unleashed, you sense he is going to come back for another. Sure enough, there he is, all over the outro. This is a great song and right for the time. The classic sing-along chorus came to be something of a mantra during the tribulations of the ensuing tour.

It was the second single from the album, backed with the first one – 'Play Ball'.

'Play Ball'
This was released as a single before the album, so it was effectively the introduction to a post-Malcolm AC/DC era. That still seemed unthinkable, but Stevie Young slotted right in. In fact, you don't really notice the switch and you can't pay him higher credit than that. It helps, of course, that this is a really strong song, easily up there with the standard of the best songs on the previous albums with Brian. It has a terrific swinging vibe, Cliff's bass provides a nice prominent pulse and the little licks that Angus plays around the rhythm are terrific.

'Rock The Blues Away'
This shares DNA with 'Anything Goes' from *Black Ice*. You have to think that this song emerged from the same sessions, which is why it fell by the wayside. It's all about the joys and fun of good times with your mates. There's a warmth and happiness to it that is infectious and a happy AC/DC song is always a good thing. It's not a great song, but it's well worth its place on the album.

It was picked as the third single released from the album in America and got to number 40.

'Miss Adventure'
The mix on this is quite dense, but then you also get the chorus of backing 'lahs' sounding like they are several rooms away. The guitar riff is nice and prominent, but this song is not an easy listen. Someone plays castanets at one

point to add more texture, but you can't hear them well. All in all, the song never takes off and is itself a misadventure.

'Dogs Of War'
Lyrically, this is one (see also 'War Machine') that dwells on more serious topics – in this case, mercenaries. Perhaps Angus had picked up a copy of Frederick Forsyth's book of the same title? The song is also reminiscent of 'War Machine' musically. The intro is a curio, with Angus sounding uncannily like Jimi Hendrix, but it soon settles down into a rolling rhythm. The chorus is one of the strongest on the album, with some great lead lines from Angus.

'Got Some Rock & Roll Thunder'
A punchy intro with glam rock overtones kicks things off before the slick, groovy riff and backing vocals come in. It's enormously catchy, with Phil's drums acting as a rock-steady thump in the heart of the mix. It's one of those where the melody in the chorus is the same as the verses, but the repeated title brings it to life. I love this song in all its stomping glory.

'Hard Times'
A count-in from Phil and we are into a slow boogie shuffle. It's not one of their best in that style and it could have done with being replaced on the album. It just isn't quite up to standard, although Angus saves it slightly by adding some fire with his burst of guitar in the outro.

'Baptism By Fire'
It harks back a little to 'Beating Around The Bush' with the twisting, stabbing riffs giving the song momentum. It has an easier groove to it than 'Beating Around The Bush', although Angus rips out a classic scorching solo that is as electric as anything he did in his twenties. They don't give him enough focus in the mix; he could have done with being pushed up a touch or two. It's a good song and worth it for that solo alone.

'Rock The House'
A solo vocal intro from Brian leads into a cascading riff. The verses are well done, with the riffs dovetailing well with Brian. There's a flavour of Zeppelin's 'Black Dog' here with the cascading riff and the stop-start rhythms. The intro riff comes back for added colour and excitement after Angus's solo. The song crackles with energy throughout and seems to end much too soon.

'Sweet Candy'
The fluttering guitar in the intro hints at Hendrix's 'Foxy Lady', and the lady this song is about seems to have a similar appeal. Whereas there's a teasing, sensuous subtlety to 'Foxy Lady', this song has broader brushstrokes. Where

it comes unstuck is the woefully dull chorus. Apart from the riff and Angus's solo, there is little here to get excited about.

'Emission Control'
It's a terrible title, although it's one you could see coming, I guess. The riff, though, is excellent, one of those tricky, detailed riffs that they do so well. It's at its best in the gang vocal choruses, with Angus wailing away to his heart's content. The fade out in the choruses and his lead playing make for a reasonable end to the album.

What Happened Next?
The tour to promote *Rock Or Bust* was dogged with personnel issues. The loss of Phil Rudd at the outset due to his criminal case was, to some extent, alleviated by the return of Chris Slade. Just when Phil probably thought things couldn't get much worse, he suffered a heart attack. He told the *Bay Of Plenty Times* in 2016 that 'I was walking around at home and I started to feel, well, just funny. I had a strange pain in my chest. So, my housekeeper took me to the hospital, where they hooked me up and did all these tests. Turned out I had a big heart attack. My artery was all blocked up and they said I had to stay in and have an operation'.

Back on the tour, things got worse when they lost Brian in March 2016 due to his hearing issues. That seemed to many observers as surely a step too far for the band to carry on with the tour. But the Youngs have always had a 'show must go on' mentality. In any case, was there really any chance the gigs could be rescheduled? So, carry on they did and, according to Chris Slade, four singers were brought in to rehearse for the gig. Chris recalled the auditions to *Ultimate Guitar* in 2022: 'Some were known and some unknown. I am sworn to secrecy about who those singers are'. One of the four was Alvi Robinson of the AC/DC tribute band Thunderstruck. This was the biggest opportunity of his life. He recounted the experience to *Brave Words* in 2021:

From what I was told, Cliff had seen me on YouTube and that was it. Their agency called my guitar player at the time and asked if I would be interested. Their next show was in Atlanta, Georgia. They were en route, on tour. My flight was about 55 minutes from Raleigh to Atlanta. We did about three hours of jamming in a rehearsal space. We started out with 'Touch Too Much' and 'Back In Black'; those were the first two we ran through, just to get a feel for everybody. Then, we just worked through the setlist.

Sadly, he didn't get the gig, and equally sadly, he also lost his day job as an HVAC (heating, ventilation and air conditioning) technician. The audition was so hush-hush, he couldn't tell his boss why he had to suddenly leave work! The man chosen for the job was already there at Atlanta. Chris Slade went on to explain:

I was told we would be having a sudden, unplanned day off, and I said, 'Why do we have a day off tomorrow? What's going on?' And they said, 'Brian can't perform. It's Axl Rose tomorrow. We need today to get ready'. So that's how quick it was. I was told that day, and then Axl turned up the next day. He came in, I shook his hand, he told a joke, and I thought, 'This guy's alright'. And when he started singing, it was unbelievable. I couldn't believe it. He sang his heart out and it was fantastic.

So, it was the high-profile Axl Rose who got the gig, and filled in brilliantly. By the end of the tour Cliff too had decided enough was enough. AC/DC were down to two regulars in Angus and Stevie, plus Chris Slade, who was unsure of what exactly his position now was.

Power Up (2020)

Personnel:
Brian Johnson: lead vocals
Angus Young: lead guitar
Stevie Young: rhythm guitar, backing vocals
Cliff Williams: bass, backing vocals
Phil Rudd: drums
Produced by Brendan O'Brien at The Warehouse, Vancouver, between August 2018 and September 2018 and Los Angeles early 2019.
Release date: 13 November 2020
Label: Columbia
Highest chart places: Australia: 1, UK: 1, USA: 1
Running time: 41:03
All songs by Angus and Malcolm Young

Malcolm's death on 18 November 2017 meant Angus was now the last remaining founding member of AC/DC. Michael Browning's personal tribute is: 'I would put Malcolm in the genius stakes. He was very underrated. A lot of people don't realise how talented he was and how crucial he was to the band. He was the conscience of the band; there's no doubt about that'.

It was apparently Malcolm's wish that Angus and the band carried on, clearly seeing the band as a job for life, a mission to keep on delivering. Angus explained to the *Sunday Post* in 2021 how the project began: 'Our management said: 'Are you thinking of doing something?' I said: 'It's time to see who wants to be back on board''. Keeping going had been difficult beyond belief, but Angus had taken on the role of band leader and made a great job of it. It was a role he had no doubt (in hindsight) co-occupied for some years. If Angus was going to make another album, he knew who had to be on it. What he needed was the only credible line-up.

Phil's place back in the scheme of things had started at Malcolm's funeral on 28 November 2017. 'I had seen Phil at Mal's funeral and he looked great', Angus told *The Guardian* in 2020. 'He told me he'd been working with these rehab people, and he still has contact with the people who were helping him. I said: 'As soon as I've got the material together, we'll hook up'.' The decision to work with Phil again didn't come as a surprise to Chris Slade. He recalled to *Ultimate Guitar* in 2022 how he was, or rather wasn't, informed:

He (Phil) ran into trouble, but I knew, based on what happened in the 1990s, that if he sorted himself out, he would maybe be back in there again. I think that, by then, I was old enough to accept things as they are. I was never told how long I might be in the band. I was never told if this was forever or if this was temporary. Obviously, I'm not in the band now, but here's the thing: I was never told, 'Oh, Slade, you're not the drummer any more'. No one in AC/DC ever called me or told me anything. Basically, the tour ended, I went home and I had no idea. I had no idea that they were making an album or if they weren't making an album. I had no idea that they had called Phil. I was just sitting at home and I knew about as much as anyone did until they announced things the way they did. There was never a point where Angus went, 'Chris, you're out and Phil is in'.

The initial call to Brian didn't come directly from Angus. 'Angus talked to the management and management got in touch with each one of us individually', Brian revealed to *The Guardian* in 2020. He also was happy to be back with the band. Cliff's retirement was due to band changes during the *Rock Or Bust* tour. It just didn't feel the same to him. But Angus must have known Cliff would likely return if he got Phil and Brian back. How could Cliff resist making another album with his old friends? Cliff was back on board, too. Also returning was Mike Fraser, who recalls that it was 'hugely emotional. After *Rock Or Bust*, I think most of us thought that was maybe the last AC/DC record, so when I got the call for *Power Up* and found out it was all the original guys back in the fold, it was an amazing feeling!'

Thus, the band regrouped to make this tribute to Malcolm. 'It was natural', Cliff told *The Guardian* in 2020. 'We've been together so long, it was not an easing-in process or anything. We obviously had to scrape some moss off, but it came together pretty quickly'. The end result is as good as could be expected, without warranting the huge acclaim some reviewers gave it. 'I think Malcolm would have been proud of this record', Angus told *The Sunday Post* in 2021. 'Some of these tracks are from around the time of *Black Ice*, the last record he played on. I said to him: 'Maybe we should try and get as much done as we can'. But he said: 'No, we'll get it later'.'

The idea was to present the new album as a complete surprise, but, says Fraser ...

... we had a terrible time trying to keep it under wraps. The whole band was trying to stay very low-key by not going out for dinners and getting room service, etc., but some paparazzi caught wind of it and for over half the record, there were people with zoom lenses surrounding the studio. Anytime one of us would go out for a smoke, the next day, it would be posted all over social media.

The material is surely, for the most part, songs and riffs that were not considered good enough for *Black Ice* or even *Rock Or Bust*. Therefore, it is astonishing that it is as good as it is. But Angus (rightly) felt proud of it and explained to *The Sunday Post* in 2021 how he had kept Malcolm close throughout.

I know he would have loved the way I put the record together for him. I was using Malcolm as a guide all the way through the recording. Anything he had done on his own, lyric-wise, I made sure I used them. I kept it the way he would have wanted it. Every time I pick up my guitar, the first thing that enters my head is, 'I think Mal will like this riff I'm playing'. That's how I judge a lot of stuff.

There is the possibility that some of the songs were new compositions by Angus alone. He undoubtedly missed his brother's input, and so did Brian, who recalled to *The Guardian* in 2020:

I was trying out singing certain lines, but it just kept flashing through my mind: 'Is this how Malcolm wants this song?' Malcolm was a strong character. He just commanded respect without even trying. And even though he's not with us anymore, he's still there. We don't want to sound gooey, but facts are facts.

Not using any of Malcolm's playing on the album is understandable, even if it were possible. For Angus, it might have felt like he was using his brother just that bit too much. However, it would have been an idea to have an ending coda of Malcolm in a more personal, distinct tribute.

Of all their albums, this was, in some ways, the most welcome release. It had been delayed by the pandemic and a new AC/DC album felt more like a gift than ever, something 'normal' back again; old friends there for us, that's how it felt. This was exactly the kind of 'power up' we needed! Sadly, there was no supporting tour and it looked like it might be a final farewell.

The album title is perfect. It embodies a band back at work and could have worked equally well for their debut. The cover is less impressive. It has a modern look and the logo looks great in the red neon style, but it doesn't resonate. The album itself is, at the very least, good, and at times it is excellent. It was really quite an achievement to pull off something of such quality. There are several AC/DC albums that don't match this one for vim and vigour and you can imagine it not being the last album for them.

On a more personal note for the band: in between the recording and release, Angus's sister Margaret Horsburgh passed away aged 84 on 11 November 2019 in New South Wales. She was such a huge support in the early years, and one suspects that she was always there for her brothers over the years.

'Realize'

The 'call to arms intro' echoes back to 'Thunderstruck', and as soon as the riff comes in, we are in even more familiar territory. It's AC/DC by numbers: good but not great. Traditionally, the first song had been the best one on the album for a while. This song isn't good enough for that role, lacking the impact and quality of its illustrious predecessor openers. It's a decent enough song but would have come over better further into the album without the track one pressure. It was the second single from the album.

'Rejection'

A sharp call and response between Angus's guitar and the rhythm trio makes for a good intro. This gritty rocker works well as track two. I love how the riff moves up the fretboard. There's nothing fancy here, but there doesn't need to be. It's an excellent song.

'Shot In The Dark'

The intro lick from Angus kicks off a fabulous rhythm, with Brian already on commanding form. The push and pull in the verses between Brian and Angus is great and the chorus is catchy. The solo is good, not great, but it does the job. Overall, it's one of the best songs on the album. It has a full-on stadium-sized roar to it in the choruses, which always goes down well. This should have been track one! It was released on 7 October 2020 as the 'teaser' single for the album.

'Through The Mists Of Time'

This track got a lot of attention in the press. It has a respectful feel in what is a heartfelt tribute to fallen brothers and friends. Brian told *The Guardian* in 2020:

> I still get goosebumps when I hear that song. I can hear Malcolm through that song. It's a throwback to the days when rock 'n' roll was so much fun and we were younger and it just seemed like nothing would end and it was always gonna be life in the early 80s, before AIDS, before all that. And when I listen to it, it's almost like time travel.

Fraser concurs, saying, 'I still tear up thinking about Mal when I hear that one'. The transition from the verses into the chorus is impressive. Just a chord change and a fill from Phil, so smoothly done. They don't overdo the chorus; it still has an element of tasteful restraint to it. The same can be said for Angus's solo, which sounds like a valedictory.

This is the best song on the album, which is interesting because it's likely to be one of the newest ones. Obviously, the lyrics are new, but you can imagine that the music was also a new creation. But if they did make use of an old, unused riff of Malcolm's, the song would take on even greater meaning. It was released for Record Store Day in June 2021 as a limited 12' picture disc single.

'Kick You When You're Down'

Another of the very best songs here, featuring a rabble-rousing blast in the chorus, which is often a good idea! It almost comes straight in on a chorus, too – there are a few scene-setting lines from Brian initially – which always helps to big a song up. The vocal arrangement is excellent, especially in the choruses, with Brian singing responses to the endearingly dispassionate backing vocal cries of 'Oh no!'. Mutt Lange might approve, but he would have gone for more melodic power on the backing vocals. The verses are a terrific contrast to the chorus, showcasing a ZZ Top feel and a great guitar melody line. And, oh my, they set up the chorus so well! This many albums in and the band can still kick out, rock and let off frustration like this. What a band!

'Witch's Spell'
The 'Shoot To Thrill' lick always means something special. Right from the intro, they have got you with that lick. And they don't drop the ball from there. The doubled rhythm guitar lines are masterful, with Angus adding some licks over the top. There in the pocket are Cliff and Phil, who make the underlying groove sound effortless. On here and throughout the album, this pair are terrific. Again, Brian is excellent; he really has hit a 'late' period hot spell with the band.

'Demon Fire'
Brian's lascivious opening salvo is superb and you can feel the enjoyment and passion in his performance throughout. The insistent, sinuous guitar riff is a gem. Brian pauses between his lines, allowing the riff to shine. The verses are engaging, but the chorus is disappointingly uninteresting. The bridge/solo section (2:15) is by far the best bit, showcasing a great detour riff and solo from Angus. As a point of trivia, Brian and the backing vocal sing 'Demon's Fire', not 'Demon Fire'.

'Wild Reputation'
This should have been bumped way higher up the album sequence. It's such a classic riff. As soon as it comes in, you have to smile with pleasure. When they latch onto a riff as great as this, it's impossible for them not to deliver. The chorus is every bit as good as you would hope, too, with the backing vocals pumped up loud. Brian gets to cover all of his bases here, from his stadium-sized vocals down to the low-down conspiratorial tone as he announces he is 'coming down Main Street, Get outta my way, I ain't stoppin' for nobody'. He means it!

'No Man's Land'
Down to earth, sadly. This sounds like the rejected tune it ultimately is. The intro riff is too shrill and would have worked a lot better in a lower key. The doubled lower harmony part when it comes in, is much better. The song picks up with the chorus, which has some bite to it, and the Phil/ Cliff rhythm duo are on form as ever, but this is a song that needed more work.

'Systems Down'
We are greeted by a surprisingly cinematic intro sounding nothing like AC/ DC, save for Phil. A jagged riff and bubbling bass work from Cliff dominate

the sound. It's a well-worked track that crackles along, with a big slamming chorus to top it off. It's another one that has been overlooked.

'Money Shot'

The intro/main riff is a bit weak, sounding like a demo workout at best. The verses are AC/DC by numbers, but the song finds depth and power in the choruses, which echo the glory years with Mutt Lange. The problem is that the main riff doesn't gell with the song; when they drop it in the choruses, the song is all the better for it.

'Code Red'

The 'Back In Black' riff lurks here, reworked in the intro. That bit of magic doesn't rub off on the rest of the track, which is sequenced last for good reason. The verses lack sparkle, but they salvage something for the chorus, though it's still too understated. Not a great finish to the album.

The Future?

There will likely be more reissues from the band and possibly, if we are lucky, new material and archive releases. We know this because of an announcement in July 2021 about the band's contract. In short, Sony Music Publishing and Alberts signed a deal about the AC/DC catalogue and that of Vanda & Young and Stevie Wright. The deal meant that the band's publishing and recording rights were brought together under the Sony banner for the first time. CEO of Alberts, David Albert, was delighted by the deal and said to *Variety* that he and the team were looking forward to working with Sony Music Publishing and continuing to create opportunities out of the catalogue.

The future, then, looks bright. Angus told *Rolling Stone* in November 2014 that AC/DC will 'keep going as long as we still feel good about it. The day you lose the heart, that's when you say, 'I can't do this any more'.'

Brian told the *Fuelling Around* podcast in May 2023 that 'It does take a lot of time to get a band like AC/DC together again. Most of the crew were out working with other people. Trying to get those guys back together again was tough, but I've got my fingers crossed that everything is going okay. The most important thing about it all is the eagerness we all feel; the juices are running again'. The first fruits of this came with the announcement that they were returning to headline at the *Power Trip* festival in October 2023. The absence of Phil Rudd for their performance raised eyebrows, with Matt Laug stepping in on drums. But it showed their intent to carry on as a live act, as well hopefully as making records.

Cliff was stated on AC/DC's X feed as coming out of retirement for *Power Trip*. A new framed picture on the band's merchandise site shows two pictures of Angus and one of Brian and Cliff. No Phil, but also, surprisingly, no Stevie. The latest rumours, as of January 2024, were that Cliff would not be there for the growing number of tour dates being revealed for later in the year.

Advancing years will obviously see the band have to call it a day, but there will also be the credibility factor as the key five members drop out for one reason or another. Having Stevie Young in for Malcolm was logical and made sense. It also kept things in the family and kept the band credible. But you feel that keeping the key five-piece line-up together is paramount. Cliff not touring could be tolerated, especially if he is still there to record. But if Phil, too, is not there for the coming tour, you have a very significant change – a whole new rhythm section.

The other issue is new material. If there is any intention of further studio albums, then where will the material come from? How many more riffs, licks and demos are left in the vault, because, surely, the best have been cherry-picked since Malcolm's departure and passing. That leaves Angus and, presumably, Stevie to come up with new tunes.

The decision on what happens will come down to Angus; it's his band. His steely resolve to keep going through the series of problems affecting the quite literal *Rock Or Bust* tour was remarkable. Michael Browning is impressed by Angus: 'Good on him, he's run with it and I really admire him. I really admire them all and their attitude, but particularly Angus. The way he's kept going in adversity – he lost George and then Malcolm. They were all really tight with each other. Malcolm was certainly the decision maker for the band and now it's Angus and he is getting things done'. Angus is a safe pair of hands and will always know in his mind what Malcolm (and George) would think and do.

The stage shows will be harder to keep going as the years pass by. For *Guitar World*, Alan Di Perna asked Angus, back in 2009, how long he thought he could keep going, given his energetic performances.

As long as I can do it and do it well. I don't want to be struggling to do it. And touring does take up a lot of your life. So when you do it, you want to do it well. If I felt I wasn't delivering, then I'd have to say, 'I can't do this any more'. You don't want to get on there in a wheelchair. But as long as I can feel it when I get on and I'm putting in that energy, I'll keep doing it.

Live Albums
Live From The Atlantic Studios (1978 and 1997)
Personnel:
Bon Scott: lead vocals
Angus Young: lead guitar
Malcolm Young: rhythm guitar, backing vocals
Cliff Williams: bass, backing vocals
Phil Rudd: drums
Produced/Remixed by George Young
Recorded at Atlantic Recording Studios, New York, 7 December 1977
Release date: April 1978 (promo), 18 November 1997 (full release)
Label: East West
Running time: 45:38

With AC/DC going down a storm on stages everywhere, it was no surprise that a live album was planned. Bon, in a letter to one Valerie Lary (dated August 1977), wrote: 'We finished our live album a few weeks ago in New York. I had to re-record about five concerts cause the vocals were not as good sound-wise as they had to be due to all the microphone spill from the guitars and things. I was alright (ahem), it sounds great and it'll look good hanging on the Xmas trees'. That live album didn't happen, but a few months later, they recorded this must-have album.

It wasn't intended for wide public consumption, and was released as a promo album by Atlantic (USA) in April 1978. The sound quality, and especially the band performance, led to it being heavily bootlegged. The album later achieved a widespread official release as part of the *Bonfire* box set, where it was remixed by George Young. When the master tape was loaded, it was noticed that the beginning of 'Live Wire' and the end of 'Rocker' were missing, so they patched in the missing audio from a vinyl album. It's a superb performance, well-recorded and essential for your collection.

If You Want Blood You've Got It (1978)
Personnel:
Bon Scott: lead vocals
Angus Young: lead guitar
Malcolm Young: rhythm guitar, backing vocals
Cliff Williams: bass, backing vocals
Phil Rudd: drums
Produced by Harry Vanda and George Young
Recorded at The Apollo Theatre, Glasgow, 30 April 1978
Label: Atlantic
Release date: 13 October 1978 (UK), 21 November 1978 (USA), 27 November 1978 (Australia). Highest chart places: Australia: 37, UK: 13, USA: 113
Running time: 52:42

Angus recalled it to *Total Guitar* in 2020 as, 'the magic show. One night, guitars out of tune, feedback, singer farting, whatever'. The idea for the record came from Atlantic and several shows were recorded so they could pick the best versions for the album. In the end, they used the Apollo gig alone.

AC/DC's third big album in a row in Europe also went Gold in America, prompting Atlantic to come up with suggestions for their further career development. The title came following an interview Angus and Bon did before their appearance at the *Day On The Green Festival* in 1978. Angus recalled to *Rolling Stone* that, 'We were on at 10:30 in the morning, and most of us hadn't even been to bed. This guy from a film crew got hold of me and Bon and asked what kind of show it was gonna be. Bon said, 'You remember when the Christians went to the lions? Well, we're the Christians'. Then, he asked me and I said, 'If they want blood, they're gonna get it'.'

Live albums were often effectively a best-of collection, a useful introduction for the curious and a great souvenir for fans. *If You Want Blood* works well on both counts. It is AC/DC at the very top of their game on the *Powerage* tour in front of a rabid 'home' Glaswegian audience. Angus recalled to the *Sunday Post* in 2021 that 'It was scary. I was watching that balcony swaying up and down. Once it started rocking in time to the music, you were hoping nothing bad was going to happen'.

George Young and Harry Vanda knew they had something special to work with as soon as they heard the tapes. Angus, again to the *Sunday Post,* recalled that 'When they got the tapes back and started listening to them, George said: 'I can even tell, just from the audio, when Angus is moving and going across the stage'. He knew where I was on the Apollo stage from just hearing it!"

In spite of the audio being so exciting, there was still some tinkering done in the studio. One track is a studio creation, while the rest will undoubtedly have been worked on to some degree. The backing vocals leap out, for example, as sounding too good for a live version. And Bon surely must have done some overdubs, judging from his past live recording comments. However, what we get is a stunning live album, even better sounding sonically than most of their studio albums!

The cover package is almost completely dominated by Angus, who is already their talisman. He's on the front with an out-of-focus Bon. Then, on the back cover, he's impaled on the stage. There being no other band pictures is unusual for a live album in those days, and something not rectified here until the digipack CD remasters series.

The vinyl and CD running order of this essential AC/DC album is: 'Riff Raff', 'Hell Aint A Bad Place To Be', 'Bad Boy Boogie', 'The Jack', 'Problem Child', 'Whole Lotta Rosie', 'Rock 'N' Roll Damnation', 'High Voltage', 'Let There Be Rock', 'Rocker'. To these, you can add 'Dog Eat Dog', which first appeared on the B-side of the 'Rosie' single and was then included on the *Backtracks* box set.

145

Those wanting a video fix of the gig will find 'Damnation', 'Dog Eat Dog', 'Let There Be Rock' and 'Bad Boy Boogie' on the *Plug Me In* box set. The *Family Jewels* set contains 'Riff Raff', 'Damnation' and 'Fling Thing'/'Rocker'.

The one 'fault' with the album is that it's only one disc; it could easily have worked as a double and the ferocity and power of the end result would not have been diminished one iota. That would have meant pulling in songs from another show and maybe they didn't have any more different songs to put in.

What makes this album so great is the commitment and power in the performance. It's there in the intro alone to 'Riff Raff' - band and audience together in unison. The explosion into the riff is intense and euphoric. You get extended, but never dull, versions of the likes of 'Bad Boy Boogie' or 'Let There Be Rock'. 'The Jack' is here with the 'proper' lyrics as it always was live.

Known musical edits and studio trickery relate to two songs. 'Rocker' was originally part of the encore at the show with 'Fling Thing' (as can be seen on *Family Jewels*). 'Fling Thing' was removed completely from the album. Then, the middle of 'Rocker' was edited out due to time constraints, and the outro was replaced completely.

If 'Rosie' has a different feel and sound to your ears compared to the rest of the album, you are right. Bon's vocal is a studio take. The difference in his voice to the rest of the album and the spot-on similarity to the studio vocals is there to be heard. The backing track sounds like a direct lift from the studio version, albeit slightly sped up to hit the same tempos and pitch as the rest of the album. A few edits are also made to the song, and another key difference is there are new solos from Angus. Whatever the Frankenstein nature of this version, it is still the one to beat – the definitive 'Rosie'.

Let There Be Rock: Live In Paris (1980)

Personnel:
Bon Scott: lead vocals
Angus Young: lead guitar
Malcolm Young: rhythm guitar, backing vocals
Cliff Williams: bass, backing vocals
Phil Rudd: drums
Mixed by Tony Platt
Recorded at Pavilion de Paris, Paris, 9 December 1979 (evening show)
Release date: 10 December 1980 (video), 17 November 1997 (Bonfire CD)
Label: East West
Highest chart places: Australia: -, UK: -, USA: -
Running time: 79:02

Using an old album title is confusing, albeit it does work well as the title of a live recording. Something unique would have made for a better title. It was first available as a video in 1980. We get to see the set-up of the show before the complete concert comes on. The recording is a little murky and grainy;

concert videos at this time were usually underlit and there were far fewer cameras at work than in recent years. While Bon is a formidable presence, it is noticeable that he has less command of the stage area than Brian Johnson. Angus carries far more of 'the act' here. Nonetheless, it's an essential video of the tour and a great performance. The video has since been made available on DVD and Blu-Ray.

The audio first achieved widespread official release as part of the *Bonfire* box set and has never been released outside of that set. The sound was recorded by Barry Ainsworth using the prestigious Rolling Stones mobile studio. The CD version has the full show, while the DVD version misses 'Rocker' and 'T.N.T'.. The audio is great quality and this remains the best record there is of a full show from the *Highway To Hell* tour, Bon's last with the band.

AC/DC Live (1992)

Personnel:
Brian Johnson: lead vocals
Angus Young: lead guitar, backing vocals
Malcolm Young: rhythm guitar, backing vocals
Cliff Williams: bass, backing vocals
Chris Slade drums
Produced by Bruce Fairbairn
Recorded on the 1991 World Tour
Release date: 26 October 1992
Label: Albert/Atco
Highest chart places: Australia: 1, UK: 5, USA: 15
Running time: 71:12 (single disc), 132:08 (double disc)

This was recorded at several shows on the *Razor's Edge* tour in 1991. The band had waited to build up material for a live album that would showcase songs from Brian's era. In spite of that, there is still a core of material from the years with Bon, although much of it was not on *If You Want Blood*.

The idea of a highlights single disc was an odd one. A studio greatest hits distilled to a single is just about understandable, but with AC/DC, surely you want the full live experience or nothing!

With all live albums, there is debate about the amount of studio overdubs that have been added. In this case, it seems likely that Angus redid some of his solos while Brian redid a lot of his vocals.

The song selection is good, with no real deep-cut surprises, although it's nice to get 'Who Made Who'. The double album and accompanying more focussed *Live At Donington* DVD/ Blu-Ray are excellent. Donington is the better choice overall, as it's one big ('Monsters Of Rock') festival gig. AC/DC are at their very best in front of such a huge crowd, and to my thinking they should have just gone with Donington for the whole live album.

They got two singles from the album in 'Highway To Hell' and 'Dirty Deeds'.

147

No Bull – Live At Madrid (1996)

Personnel:
Brian Johnson: lead vocals
Angus Young: lead guitar, backing vocals
Malcolm Young: rhythm guitar, backing vocals
Cliff Williams: bass, backing vocals
Phil Rudd: drums
Mixed by Mike Fraser
Recorded at Plaza de Toros de Las Ventas, Madrid, 10 July 1996
Release date: 19 November 1996 (VHS), 16 October 2000 (DVD), 16 September 2008 (Blu-Ray)
Label: East West
Running time: 120:00

The film was directed by David Mallet and recorded on the *Ballbreaker* tour. The director's cut has two additional goodies in the form of rare outings recorded on the tour: 'Cover You In Oil' (Gothenburg) and 'Down Payment Blues' (Daytona Beach).

Although it's been released in three formats now, they have still managed to resist releasing a CD version. The footage is electric and this is a must-have video of AC/DC in concert. 'For Those About To Rock' alone is worth the price of purchase, while hardcore fans can also delight in an outing for 'Dog Eat Dog'.

Stiff Upper Lip Live (2001)

Personnel:
Brian Johnson: lead vocals
Angus Young: lead guitar, backing vocals
Malcolm Young: rhythm guitar, backing vocals
Cliff Williams: bass, backing vocals
Phil Rudd: drums
Produced by George Young
Engineered and mixed by Mike Fraser
Recorded at Olympiastadion, Munich, 14 June 2001
Release date: 4 December 2001
Label: East West
Running time: 140:00

AC/DC and a pumped-up Munich crowd make for a great concert. It's a mystery why it hasn't had a CD or vinyl release. The song selection features 'Problem Child' and 'Up To My Neck In You' as surprise deep-cut inclusions. Only the title track makes it here from 'Stiff Upper Lip', though others were played at different dates on the tour. It's an essential tour souvenir. This is the concert I come back to and watch again most often.

Live At River Plate (2011)
Personnel:
Brian Johnson: lead vocals
Angus Young: lead guitar, backing vocals
Malcolm Young: rhythm guitar, backing vocals
Cliff Williams: bass, backing vocals
Phil Rudd: drums
Recorded by Mike Fraser at River Plate Stadium, Buenos Aires, 2 – 6 December 2009
Release date: 10 May 2011 (DVD, Blu-Ray), 19 November 2012 (CD)
Label: Albert/Atco
Highest chart places: Australia: 11, UK: 14, USA: 66
Running time: 111:48 (DVD, Blu-Ray), 111:00 (CD)

This came out as the souvenir video of a *Black Ice* tour concert. Unusually for AC/DC, it was also later released as a double CD. The mix is noticeably different, much fuller, on the CD in comparison to the video. The CD is also taken only from the 4 December show, while the video was taken from all three shows. The band are on fire and the Buenos Aires crowd match them for energy all the way. They sing along to the riffs as much as they do the lyrics!

As an album, it hangs together well. It's the classic Brian-era line-up playing a classic setlist. The *Black Ice* album is represented by 'Rock 'N' Roll Train', 'Big Jack', 'Black Ice' and 'War Machine'. 'Rock 'N' Roll Train' is great, but the other three were not strong enough in the set. If they were hell-bent on more from *Black Ice,* then 'Skies On Fire' and 'Rocking All The Way' would have been better inclusions. 'Hard As A Rock' or 'Heatseeker' would have improved the back catalogue representation.

There are so many highlights, but standouts from a hardcore fan's point of view would include 'Hell Ain't A Bad Place To Be' and 'Dog Eat Dog', both being Bon deep cuts in the later Brian years. Notice how it's the Bon songs that kept cropping up as deep cuts on these live releases, with the band never resurrecting any oldies from Brian's era. 'Shoot To Thrill' was released as a single from the album.

149

Compilation Albums and Film Soundtracks

The soundtrack to *Iron Man 2* is an interesting compilation of AC/DC songs and a pretty good overview for the curious or casual purchaser. But it has nothing new to offer, unlike the following boxes of goodies.

Who Made Who

Personnel:
Brian Johnson: lead vocals
Angus Young: lead guitar
Malcolm Young: rhythm guitar, backing vocals
Cliff Williams: bass, backing vocals
Simon Wright: drums
New songs produced at Compass Point Studios between December 1985 and January 1986 by Harry Vanda and George Young
Release date: 26 May 1986
Label: Albert/Atlantic
Highest chart places: Australia: 30, UK: 16, USA: 33
Running time: 37:50
Songs: 'Who Made Who', 'You Shook Me All Night Long', 'D. T.', 'Sink The Pink', 'Ride On', 'Hells Bells', 'Shake Your Foundations', 'Chase The Ace', 'For Those About To Rock'

When Stephen King got the green light to direct a film based on his own short story, *Trucks*, he knew exactly who he wanted for the soundtrack. King persuaded AC/DC to supply key songs from their back catalogue, as well as write a completely new song and compose new instrumental backing tracks and cues. It wasn't an obvious fit, to be honest, but the band did themselves enormous credit with *Maximum Overdrive*, pulling it off well.

After the average *Fly On The Wall*, the band needed something to reignite their career. Having Harry and George back was a huge help, as was the running order with some choice old favourites along with three new tracks. The old songs were actually personally picked by Stephen King.

'Shake Your Foundations' is edited down from 4:10 to 3:53 and George Young manages to considerably improve the mix so we can hear Brian better. He holds the drums back, too, to create a real impact when they come in. These simple tweaks elevate the song in stature – it's a must-hear in this edit!

The other track that stands out most in the old material is 'Ride On', which is the only one with Bon and not an obvious choice. Its inclusion did a lot for the song's belated recognition as a classic. There are also some cues and set pieces that didn't make the soundtrack. They are extremely well done and all are easy to find online.

'Who Made Who'

This is one of their best songs in the 'between Phil Rudd' era. A powerful 4/4 rhythm from Simon and Cliff is the bedrock, with Malcolm's cutting rhythm guitar. The chorus is a huge, swelling roar that really sells the song in such a positive way. Another big plus is from Angus, who goes in for some Eddie Van Halen-style tapping on his solo. Lyrically, it's way outside the band's usual oeuvre and is written to order, being a broad outline of the film's plot, which sees machines taking over the world. There is a superior extended 12' version, but the 7' is also good. It got to 16 in the UK singles and 23 in America.

'D. T.'

This is excellent. Who would have expected the Youngs to come up with such a highly credible piece of instrumental music for a soundtrack? It has great dynamics and there's this effective technique of shifting between a clean and distorted tone. Angus's solo is a real screamer. The outro is just superb; the cooling-off tones are a real delight, an unusual ending for AC/DC. Frustratingly, you can hear Angus audibly coming back in as the song fades out.

'Chase The Ace'

This is a high-tempo blaster of an instrumental, with Simon doing a fair approximation of what Phil Rudd might have played. Angus gets in a deranged wild solo for nearly all the second half of the song. He is just astounding, really letting rip and keeping going as the band play on behind him.

The Last Action Hero
'Big Gun' (Angus and Malcolm Young)
Release Date: 25 June 1993
Label: Atco

AC/DC (still with Chris Slade on drums) performed this specially written song for the soundtrack of the *Last Action Hero* film starring Arnold Schwarzenegger. It sees them make a strong return to their earlier sound, being a solid, blues-based rocker with a boogie-style verse and some swinging lead playing from Angus. It was recorded in early 1993 with Rick Rubin producing. He impressed the band enough to get the gig to produce their next album.

The main riff is vintage AC/DC and the band deliver the song well. The chorus isn't quite strong enough, let down by the title, which just doesn't pop out at you. It was released as successful single, helped by a great video with Schwarzenegger appearing dressed like Angus and performing the guitarist's duck walk next to him. They didn't record a B-side or extra tracks; therefore, around the world, a variety of unreleased live tracks were used, all available on *Backtracks*. The song has somewhat slipped under the radar.

Bonfire
Release date: 18 November 1997
Label: East West

This superb box set was intended to mark what would have been Bon's 50th birthday in 1996. The usual production travails saw it emerge a year late. It was a CD-only release comprising five discs, including two live albums, a rarities disc titled *Volts* and a remastered *Back In Black*.

The inclusion of *Back In Black* was a surprise. While the intentions were obviously well-meaning, it still feels like the wrong decision. The way to go, instead, was surely a 'best of' Bon set.

The live albums – *Atlantic Studios 1977* and *Paris 1979* – are detailed in the live section of this book. The studio tracks from *Volts* are all commented on under the relevant parent albums. The otherwise scarce live tracks are: 'Sin City' (*Midnight Special*, 1978) and 'She's Got Balls' (*Bondi Lifesaver*, 1977). The latter was also a B-side to 'You Shook Me All Night Long'.

Family Jewels
Release date: 28 March 2005
Label: Albert/Epic
This DVD compilation covers the Bon years (disc one) and the Brian years (disc two), which is convenient, although obviously unbalanced. The selection of promo videos and live and studio clips is always entertaining and the set is well worth getting. The third part was later included on *Backtracks* – a better idea might have been to reissue *Family Jewels* as a three-disc set.

Plug Me In
Release date: 16 October 2007
Label: Albert/Columbia
This DVD box set anthology is an essential purchase. This also divides the Bon and Brian eras onto different discs, but disc three, *Between The Cracks*, is a curious decision. This is an 'extras' disc, but some of the material is from the same sources as on discs one and two! It's ridiculous not to keep the material together, even though it would have meant disc two being 50/50 Bon and Brian, bumping the rest of Brian to disc three. That aside, this is still a glorious live record of AC/DC.

Backtracks
Release date: 10 November 2009
Label: Columbia
This superb box set gathers up studio rarities and a huge number of live tracks. The first CD is the studio material. The second and third CDs are otherwise unreleased live material. Also included is the third part of the *Family Jewels* promo videos. If you were flush with cash (it's now unavailable), you could buy the deluxe version that had a working guitar amp and various bits of paraphernalia. For collectors, the main additional interest to it was an otherwise unavailable full performance on DVD of a show at Circus Krone, Munich, on 17 June 2003, as well as a vinyl album of studio rarities. Circus Krone has since leaked out into the wider market as a bootleg copy on DVD and MP3.

Appendix 1: Selling The Brand – Gerard Huerta

Think of AC/DC and the logo is right there in your head. In fact, that logo is everywhere, on all manner of consumer products. The man who came up with it is Gerard Huerta, who started creating logos in 1974. His work straddles music and the wider leisure, retail and business industries. He is the man who designed logos for Blue Öyster Cult, Boston, Foreigner, Ted Nugent and many other bands, but the best and most enduring is his iconic logo for AC/DC, which has emblazoned every AC/DC product (bar the *Powerage* era) since *Let There Be Rock* was released.

Huerta is amazed at the longevity of his work. 'I was very young, so I was happy to do the work and it was great. I got paid well for everything I did. I don't think anyone would ever have thought that any of this stuff would hold any kind of value or use in the future. At the time, it was seen as ephemera – it was done, it was out, it was gone'. But Huerta still sees the benefits of his design:

The value in having done that lettering has allowed me to do a lot of other things. A typical case would be this: a DJ called Don Imus, a famous shock-jock, called me and the first words out of his mouth before he hired me was, 'Did you do the AC/DC logo?' So I said 'Yes', and he said, 'Okay, I wanna hire you'. In the last couple of years, I have done five or six band logos for people who are a throwback to the 1970s.

Huerta first worked on lettering for the international *High Voltage* cover, with Angus on the cover.

I had been working at CBS and one of the nice things about album cover design is you get a credit on the album. You know other art directors are seeing this. I went freelance in 1976 and Bob Defrin (art director) at Atlantic Records was one of those who noted I had done a lot of lettering. He called me in to do a few sketches for *High Voltage* and he chose one. So, I inked it without having seen the cover at all. A lot of times, that would happen. This was essentially a lettering design to be plonked on it. I must have known it was going on the top left because I remember ruling out those horizontal lines that would bleed off on either side.

I had all these letters made out of lightning bolts and they're very unusual. I always start with a drawing; I do sketches and check off the ones that I like. The execution process used to be ink and airbrush, paint, overlay film – all these different techniques.

He continues:

The artwork was done in black and white line and the colours were called out mechanically to go with the photo illustration. AC/DC had used a lightning bolt with some typography, and, if I recall correctly, I was told to

put that in there. I don't know what the band thought of it. I didn't know
AC/DC from anybody; they were essentially a new group in the United
States.

Huerta was called back to design the now-iconic logo for *Let There Be Rock*.

I did three different sketches for it. That happened to be the one that was
selected, so I coloured it. I went for the orange colour because it would
look nice on the blue background. I bevel-edged it so that it would be very
legible. I still have my original artwork and it's not in too bad condition. The
starbursts aren't there because they were put on with an acetate overlay.
I didn't do the album title; it was probably Bob Defrin who set the type,
which is a very traditional serif Roman face.

Huerta still has never heard from the band about his logo.

It is funny that we have the logo in common, and yet I have never spoken
to them. I don't expect I ever will, either. Back then, you would do sketches
and show them a final drawing. Then, you would do the actual final design
and that would be an end to it. The difference for companies like Hipgnosis
or Pacific Eye & Ear is that they were probably working with the group. I
never did; I always had a middle-man – an art director or a creative director.
Then, a lot of these things would be for a first or early album, so the band
didn't have a lot of input. We would be left to our own devices to come up
with something we thought was cool.

The logo was 'dropped' for *Powerage* but returned for good with *If You Want
Blood*. Huerta was surprised it came back, commenting, 'You had new logos
being developed all the time for groups. I don't think I was even aware
it came back at the time. I was slowly working my way out of the record
business, so I was not following it as much'. As it was reused on successive
covers, there were tweaks made to the logo, including colour and size. Huerta
says:

My only thought on the logo being adapted is a technical lettering problem.
If you look at the letters AC/DC, you have points at the top with the
exception of the 'D', and you have points at the bottom with the exception
of the 'D'. Now, as a lettering person, you understand that any time you have
a point or a curve, it goes above or below the baseline. It has to because
otherwise, visually, it looks smaller. One of the things that has been done in
redrawing the logo is they've made a guideline at the top – the points go to
the guideline and also, the straight top of the 'D' is on the guideline, so the
'D' always looks too big. It's more obvious if you look at the bottom; the 'C'
lines up with the bottom of the 'D' and it really should be lower than that.

But why change it at all?

Someone down the line must have said, 'This guy didn't know what he was doing; he's made the 'D' too small'. But I did know what I was doing, so visually, when you look at it, it all appears the same size. The other thing is the way the lightning bolt touches the 'C' and the 'D'. That was carefully orchestrated so that the bevel would work; it's a very subtle thing. But I notice that in some of the re-drawings of it, the lightning bolt gets longer, and it doesn't touch in the right places. It's been fussed with a little bit.

Huerta's logo has proliferated over the decades.

They realised the logo was a graphic that was 'them', and by using the graphic, it would imply the band. They have been very good at just pounding it over and over again. I see little kids here walking around town in AC/DC shirts and hats and whatever. It's fascinating and it's because of the tremendous amount of exposure that the logo has received through the band marketing it.

Appendix 2: Stevie Wright's Solo Albums

The former Easybeats vocalist's two seventies albums, *Hard Road* (1974) and *Black Eyed Bruiser* (1975) are produced and largely written by his ex-bandmates Vanda and Young. Both albums have some excellent songs on them and have AC/DC links.

Hard Road's band is Harry Vanda (guitar), Malcolm Young (guitar), George Young (bass), John Proud (drums) and Warren Morgan (piano). Best of the lot is the three-part 'Evie', which is absolutely magnificent – an 11-minute epic moving from rock ('Let Your Hair Down') to ballad ('Evie') and finally into Tamla Motown territory ('I'm Losing You'). Tony Currenti plays the drums on 'I'm Losing You', and you get Malcolm's killer solo and fills on 'Let Your Hair Down'.

The core band on *Black Eyed Bruiser* is Harry Vanda (guitar), George Young (bass, piano, percussion), Tony Currenti (who plays most of the drums) and Malcolm Young (guitar). Currenti says: 'It was the same thing (as on *High Voltage*), they had a drummer, Johnny Dick his name was, and he recorded a couple of tracks and then he started touring with John Paul Young. So, George used me to finish off the album. Harry was the lead guitarist, but Malcolm got used on a couple of songs. Harry was the main player because I recorded with George and Harry'.

The title track is the best song and one for all AC/DC fans. It gives you a good idea of what Wright might have been like with AC/DC. The powerful, crunching riff sounds like Malcolm and there's a fabulous breakdown section featuring George's piano over the tight rhythm track.

On Track Series

Allman Brothers Band – Andrew Wild 978-1-78952-252-5
Tori Amos – Lisa Torem 978-1-78952-142-9
Aphex Twin – Beau Waddell 978-1-78952-267-9
Asia – Peter Braidis 978-1-78952-099-6
Badfinger – Robert Day-Webb 978-1-878952-176-4
Barclay James Harvest – Keith And Monica Domone 978-1-78952-067-5
Beck – Arthur Lizie 978-1-78952-258-7
The Beatles – Andrew Wild 978-1-78952-009-5
The Beatles Solo 1969-1980 – Andrew Wild 978-1-78952-030-9
Blue Oyster Cult – Jacob Holm-Lupo 978-1-78952-007-1
Blur – Matt Bishop 978-178952-164-1
Marc Bolan And T.rex – Peter Gallagher 978-1-78952-124-5
Kate Bush – Bill Thomas 978-1-78952-097-2
Camel – Hamish Kuzminski 978-1-78952-040-8
Captain Beefheart – Opher Goodwin 978-1-78952 235-8
Caravan – Andy Boot 978-1-78952-127-6
Cardiacs – Eric Benac 978-1-78952-131-3
Nick Cave And The Bad Seeds – Dominic Sanderson 978-1-78952-240-2
Eric Clapton Solo – Andrew Wild 978-1-78952-141-2
The Clash – Nick Assirati 978-1-78952-077-4
Elvis Costello And The Attractions – Georg Purvis 978-1-78952-129-0
Crosby, Stills & Nash – Andrew Wild 978-1-78952-039-2
Creedence Clearwater Revival – Tony Thompson 978-178952-237-2
The Damned – Morgan Brown 978-1-78952-136-8
Deep Purple And Rainbow 1968-79 – Steve Pilkington 978-1-78952-002-6
Dire Straits – Andrew Wild 978-1-78952-044-6
The Doors – Tony Thompson 978-1-78952-137-5
Dream Theater – Jordan Blum 978-1-78952-050-7
Eagles – John Van Der Kiste 978-1-78952-260-0
Earth, Wind And Fire – Bud Wilkins 978-1-78952-272-3
Electric Light Orchestra – Barry Delve 978-1-78952-152-8
Emerson Lake And Palmer – Mike Goode 978-1-78952-000-2
Fairport Convention – Kevan Furbank 978-1-78952-051-4
Peter Gabriel – Graeme Scarfe 978-1-78952-138-2
Genesis – Stuart Macfarlane 978-1-78952-005-7
Gentle Giant – Gary Steel 978-1-78952-058-3
Gong – Kevan Furbank 978-1-78952-082-8
Green Day – William E. Spevack 978-1-78952-261-7
Hall And Oates – Ian Abrahams 978-1-78952-167-2
Hawkwind – Duncan Harris 978-1-78952-052-1
Peter Hammill – Richard Rees Jones 978-1-78952-163-4
Roy Harper – Opher Goodwin 978-1-78952-130-6
Jimi Hendrix – Emma Stott 978-1-78952-175-7
The Hollies – Andrew Darlington 978-1-78952-159-7
Horslips – Richard James 978-1-78952-263-1
The Human League And The Sheffield Scene –
Andrew Darlington 978-1-78952-186-3
The Incredible String Band – Tim Moon 978-1-78952-107-8
Iron Maiden – Steve Pilkington 978-1-78952-061-3
Joe Jackson – Richard James 978-1-78952-189-4
Jefferson Airplane – Richard Butterworth 978-1-78952-143-6
Jethro Tull – Jordan Blum 978-1-78952-016-3
Elton John In The 1970s – Peter Kearns 978-1-78952-034-7
Billy Joel – Lisa Torem 978-1-78952-183-2
Judas Priest – John Tucker 978-1-78952-018-7

Kansas – Kevin Cummings 978-1-78952-057-6
The Kinks – Martin Hutchinson 978-1-78952-172-6
Korn – Matt Karpe 978-1-78952-153-5
Led Zeppelin – Steve Pilkington 978-1-78952-151-1
Level 42 – Matt Philips 978-1-78952-102-3
Little Feat – Georg Purvis - 978-1-78952-168-9
Aimee Mann – Jez Rowden 978-1-78952-036-1
Joni Mitchell – Peter Kearns 978-1-78952-081-1
The Moody Blues – Geoffrey Feakes 978-1-78952-042-2
Motorhead – Duncan Harris 978-1-78952-173-3
Nektar – Scott Meze – 978-1-78952-257-0
New Order – Dennis Remmer – 978-1-78952-249-5
Nightwish – Simon Mcmurdo – 978-1-78952-270-9
Laura Nyro – Philip Ward 978-1-78952-182-5
Mike Oldfield – Ryan Yard 978-1-78952-060-6
Opeth – Jordan Blum 978-1-78-952-166-5
Pearl Jam – Ben L. Connor 978-1-78952-188-7
Tom Petty – Richard James 978-1-78952-128-3
Pink Floyd – Richard Butterworth 978-1-78952-242-6
The Police – Pete Braidis 978-1-78952-158-0
Porcupine Tree – Nick Holmes 978-1-78952-144-3
Queen – Andrew Wild 978-1-78952-003-3
Radiohead – William Allen 978-1-78952-149-8
Rancid – Paul Matts 989-1-78952-187-0
Renaissance – David Detmer 978-1-78952-062-0
Reo Speedwagon – Jim Romag 978-1-78952-262-4
The Rolling Stones 1963-80 – Steve Pilkington 978-1-78952-017-0
The Smiths And Morrissey – Tommy Gunnarsson 978-1-78952-140-5
Spirit – Rev. Keith A. Gordon – 978-1-78952- 248-8
Stackridge – Alan Draper 978-1-78952-232-7
Status Quo The Frantic Four Years – Richard James 978-1-78952-160-3
Steely Dan – Jez Rowden 978-1-78952-043-9
Steve Hackett – Geoffrey Feakes 978-1-78952-098-9
Tears For Fears – Paul Clark - 978-178952-238-9
Thin Lizzy – Graeme Stroud 978-1-78952-064-4
Tool – Matt Karpe 978-1-78952-234-1
Toto – Jacob Holm-Lupo 978-1-78952-019-4
U2 – Eoghan Lyng 978-1-78952-078-1
Ufo – Richard James 978-1-78952-073-6
Van Der Graaf Generator – Dan Coffey 978-1-78952-031-6
Van Halen – Morgan Brown – 9781-78952-256-3
The Who – Geoffrey Feakes 978-1-78952-076-7
Roy Wood And The Move – James R Turner 978-1-78952-008-8
Yes – Stephen Lambe 978-1-78952-001-9
Frank Zappa 1966 To 1979 – Eric Benac 978-1-78952-033-0
Warren Zevon – Peter Gallagher 978-1-78952-170-2
10cc – Peter Kearns 978-1-78952-054-5

Decades Series
The Bee Gees In The 1960s – Andrew Mon Hughes Et Al 978-1-78952-148-1
The Bee Gees In The 1970s – Andrew Mon Hughes Et Al 978-1-78952-179-5
Black Sabbath In The 1970s – Chris Sutton 978-1-78952-171-9
Britpop – Peter Richard Adams And Matt Pooler 978-1-78952-169-6
Phil Collins In The 1980s – Andrew Wild 978-1-78952-185-6
Alice Cooper In The 1970s – Chris Sutton 978-1-78952-104-7
Alice Cooper In The 1980s – Chris Sutton 978-1-78952-259-4

Curved Air In The 1970s – Laura Shenton 978-1-78952-069-9
Donovan In The 1960s – Jeff Fitzgerald 978-1-78952-233-4
Bob Dylan In The 1980s – Don Klees 978-1-78952-157-3
Brian Eno In The 1970s – Gary Parsons 978-1-78952-239-6
Faith No More In The 1990s – Matt Karpe 978-1-78952-250-1
Fleetwood Mac In The 1970s – Andrew Wild 978-1-78952-105-4
Fleetwood Mac In The 1980s – Don Klees 978-178952-254-9
Focus In The 1970s – Stephen Lambe 978-1-78952-079-8
Free And Bad Company In The 1970s – John Van Der Kiste 978-1-78952-178-8
Genesis In The 1970s – Bill Thomas 978178952-146-7
George Harrison In The 1970s – Eoghan Lyng 978-1-78952-174-0
Kiss In The 1970s – Peter Gallagher 978-1-78952-246-4
Manfred Mann's Earth Band In The 1970s – John Van Der Kiste 978178952-243-3
Marillion In The 1980s – Nathaniel Webb 978-1-78952-065-1
Van Morrison In The 1970s – Peter Childs - 978-1-78952-241-9
Mott The Hoople And Ian Hunter In The 1970s – John Van Der Kiste 978-1-78-952-162-7
Pink Floyd In The 1970s – Georg Purvis 978-1-78952-072-9
Suzi Quatro In The 1970s – Darren Johnson 978-1-78952-236-5
Queen In The 1970s – James Griffiths 978-1-78952-265-5
Roxy Music In The 1970s – Dave Thompson 978-1-78952-180-1
Slade In The 1970s – Darren Johnson 978-1-78952-268-6
Status Quo In The 1980s – Greg Harper 978-1-78952-244-0
Tangerine Dream In The 1970s – Stephen Palmer 978-1-78952-161-0
The Sweet In The 1970s – Darren Johnson 978-1-78952-139-9
Uriah Heep In The 1970s – Steve Pilkington 978-1-78952-103-0
Van Der Graaf Generator In The 1970s – Steve Pilkington 978-1-78952-245-7
Rick Wakeman In The 1970s – Geoffrey Feakes 978-1-78952-264-8
Yes In The 1980s – Stephen Lambe With David Watkinson 978-1-78952-125-2

On Screen Series
Carry On... – Stephen Lambe 978-1-78952-004-0
David Cronenberg – Patrick Chapman 978-1-78952-071-2
Doctor Who: The David Tennant Years – Jamie Hailstone 978-1-78952-066-8
James Bond – Andrew Wild 978-1-78952-010-1
Monty Python – Steve Pilkington 978-1-78952-047-7
Seinfeld Seasons 1 To 5 – Stephen Lambe 978-1-78952-012-5

Other Books
1967: A Year In Psychedelic Rock 978-1-78952-155-9
1970: A Year In Rock – John Van Der Kiste 978-1-78952-147-4
1973: The Golden Year Of Progressive Rock 978-1-78952-165-8
Babysitting A Band On The Rocks – G.d. Praetorius 978-1-78952-106-1
Eric Clapton Sessions – Andrew Wild 978-1-78952-177-1
Derek Taylor: For Your Radioactive Children – Andrew Darlington 978-1-78952-038-5
The Golden Road: The Recording History Of The Grateful Dead – John Kilbride 978-1-78952-156-6
Iggy And The Stooges On Stage 1967-1974 – Per Nilsen 978-1-78952-101-6
Jon Anderson And The Warriors – The Road To Yes – David Watkinson 978-1-78952-059-0
Magic: The David Paton Story – David Paton 978-1-78952-266-2
Misty: The Music Of Johnny Mathis – Jakob Baekgaard 978-1-78952-247-1
Nu Metal: A Definitive Guide – Matt Karpe 978-1-78952-063-7
Tommy Bolin: In And Out Of Deep Purple – Laura Shenton 978-1-78952-070-5
Maximum Darkness – Deke Leonard 978-1-78952-048-4
The Twang Dynasty – Deke Leonard 978-1-78952-049-1

And Many More To Come!

Would you like to write for Sonicbond Publishing?

At Sonicbond Publishing we are always on the look-out for authors, particularly for our two main series:

On Track. Mixing fact with in depth analysis, the On Track series examines the work of a particular musical artist or group. All genres are considered from easy listening and jazz to 60s soul to 90s pop, via rock and metal.

On Screen. This series looks at the world of film and television. Subjects considered include directors, actors and writers, as well as entire television and film series. As with the On Track series, we balance fact with analysis.

While professional writing experience would, of course, be an advantage the most important qualification is to have real enthusiasm and knowledge of your subject. First-time authors are welcomed, but the ability to write well in English is essential.

Sonicbond Publishing has distribution throughout Europe and North America, and all books are also published in E-book form. Authors will be paid a royalty based on sales of their book.

Further details are available from www.sonicbondpublishing.co.uk. To contact us, complete the contact form there or email info@sonicbondpublishing.co.uk